C000067350

The

Châzôwn

Daniel's vision of the Ram and He-goat

A Systematic Study

By D. Wayne Davidson

How long *shall be* the vision *concerning* the daily
sacrifice, and the transgression of desolation, to
give both the sanctuary and the host to be trodden
under foot? Daniel 8:13.

FIRST EDITION

Copyright © 2022 D. Wayne Davidson

All rights reserved. No portion of this book may be reproduced by any means, graphic, electronic, or mechanical, including photocopying, recording, taping or by any information storage retrieval system without permission from the publisher, except as permitted by U.S. copyright law. For permissions contact: TheEschatonSeries@yahoo.com

Printed by Kindle Desktop Publishing in the United States of America

First Printing 2022

Preface

The Scriptures have ever been my delight and my intrigue, especially the apocalyptic books of Daniel and Revelation. Frankly, I believe what is written in its pages is that which God hath intended and ordained for each, and every generation. Each generation must therefore search the Scriptures to determine just what the God of heaven is communicating to them for the times in which they live.

During my graduate study years, I became acutely aware of the results of modern critical commentary on the Scriptures and struggled to find a bridge that would connect "thus sayeth the LORD" to these complex findings of such scholars. The more I gave myself to the study of these complex and critical works, the more questions I had regarding the authenticity of the Word of God. Eventually, a slow acute reality began to dawn. These critical works disparaged fundamental understanding associated with the Scriptures. They evaluated the primitive words and works of shepherds, farmers and fishermen, against a stratagem that they themselves had labored a lifetime to construct and then declared that the words and works of these individuals who had honestly labored for the LORD did not measure up to the system that these scholars had constructed as truth.

From the dawn of the modern era, there has been a continued denigration of the Word of God by critical scholars. However, many of these individuals are avowed skeptics, deists, agnostics and atheists, as they do not themselves believe in predictive prophecy; yet these are the "scholars," whose works are the most read and referenced in our theological institutions across Christendom.

Stayed on this trajectory, the words of Isaiah become evident:

> *Isa29:11 And the vision of all is become unto you as the words of a book that is sealed, which men deliver to one that is learned, saying, Read this, I pray thee: and he saith, I cannot; for it is sealed: 12 and the book is delivered to him that is not learned, saying, Read this, I pray thee: and he saith, I am not learned.*

This study that you are holding in your hand is the first in a series. Using the Bible, history and Strong's concordance along with a healthy dose of the Holy Spirit, the intent is to study the Word of God and accept it as authentic and authoritative, while, at the same time determining its validity against today's critical commentary. I pray God's richest blessing as you avail yourself to this study of God's Word.

Table of Contents

1: Introduction

Have you ever played the game, telephone? This is actually a socially interactive icebreaker for large gatherings. It starts with the first individual whispering a simple sentence in the ear of the person next to them. The sentence cannot be one that is complicated. An example of a sentence that can be used would be: *My neighbor has a brown cat.* Each succeeding person, after listening to what was whispered in their ear, whispers in the ear of the next person what they heard, and the game continues until the last person says out loud what they have heard. The final sentence is usually hilariously different from the original.

What does this game have to do with this study of the *châzôwn?* As we come closer to the end of time and the Second Coming of Jesus, there are individuals who are honest seekers of truth. They are trying to examine what they believe against what they are hearing, in the pulpit, in the media and in the many YouTube videos that are ever ready to captivate its audience. These honest seekers of truth will follow truth, once, with the guidance of the Holy Spirit it resonates as truth. The *châzôwn* is not so much about examining what critical scholars have documented; but it is more about looking at the truth recorded in the writings of Daniel that is relevant for our times.

In today's eschatological circles, there are so many and varied approaches and interpretations of Daniel that this might seem to be just another book on Daniel; however, this work is markedly different for the following reasons:

This is more of a study than a book. It is a study that is presented in a book format. This work goes beyond the present author's views to an examination of the actual intent of the original writing. While we, in our English language use our punctuation and syntax to ensure that proper communication takes place, in the original writing of Daniel, such punctuations were not present. We must therefore look at the construction of the text, the flow of the narrative and the original word usage in order to determine the author's true intent.

When listening to today's varied eschatological views, it sounds as though we are at the end of the telephone game. It is remarkable to know that all these views come from the same original writing! The *châzôwn* is therefore about sifting through these various methodologies,[1] returning to the original writings, determining just what was actually conveyed, to determine if today's eschatological views are sustainable based on a correct understanding of this important vision of Daniel.

Why is this study important to the honest seeker of truth? As we come closer to the Second Coming of Jesus Christ, there are many who are honestly looking for and hoping that they will be caught up to meet the LORD in the air. They have an intense dread regarding receiving the Mark of the Beast and worshiping the Antichrist. Yet, these seekers of truth have not as yet determined just what the Mark of the Beast is, nor do they conclusively know the identity of Antichrist. To these individuals, I strongly recommend that they begin their search by observing the words of Jesus in Matthew 24:15 *Study Daniel!*

---

[1] Note: These various methodologies include, Preterism, Historicism, Idealism and Futurism with its corollary of Dispensationalism.

2: Why Begin in Daniel?

In the eighth chapter of the book of Daniel, the author writes:

> *Dan8:1 In the third year of the reign of king Belshazzar a vision appeared unto me, even unto me Daniel, after that which appeared unto me at the first. ² And I saw in a vision; and it came to pass, when I saw, that I was at Shushan in the palace, which is in the province of Elam; and I saw in a vision, and I was by the river of Ulai.*

In the original language Daniel uses the word *châzôwn* to reference this vision; however, in Chapter 7 he uses a different word, *chêzêv*, to reference that vision:

> *Dan7:1 In the first year of Belshazzar king of Babylon Daniel had a dream and visions of his head upon his bed: then he wrote the dream, and told the sum of the matters. ² Daniel spake and said, I saw in my vision by night, and, behold, the four winds of the heaven strove upon the great sea.*

To the casual English reader of these passages, the significance of Daniel's usage of these different words for "vision", *châzôwn* vs *chêzêv*, might be insignificant; however, it must be brought to mind that Daniel is a scholar as he was schooled in the very best university of his day. The words he uses, and the construction of his work must be accepted as that which was not only divinely presented; but, intellectually documented. Therefore, to the honest seeker of biblical truth the usage of these different words makes a monumental difference as he follows the divine directive:

> *2 Tim2:15 Study to shew thyself approved unto God, a workman that needeth not to be ashamed, rightly dividing the word of truth.*

There is a real chasm between reading the Scripture and studying the Scripture. Here the apostle Paul equates the earnest seeker to a workman who rightly divides the word of truth. It must be pointed out that the Bible was originally written in Aramaic, Hebrew and Greek. Any other language would constitute a third-party translation of these languages. In order to unearth the truth, the honest workman must therefore look at the original languages of the Bible.[2] To unearth these gems of biblical truths from the Word of God, this workman must acquire the tools of perseverance, diligence, an open mind and a healthy dose of the Holy Spirit.

The book of Daniel has continued to intrigue many. There are those who come with a preconceived notion in search of content to bolster that which they have already believed. Others follow the path of academic criticism, decrying that the book was written in the 6th century BC, by a Hebrew captive in Babylon, while a few follow the text itself. Interestingly, it is the few who Jesus say finds truth:

> *Matt7:13 Enter ye in at the strait gate: for wide is the gate, and broad is the way, that leadeth to destruction, and many there be which go in thereat: 14 because strait is the gate, and narrow is the way, which leadeth unto life, and few there be that find it.*

When it comes to biblical truth, no one wants to be deceived or to accept that what they have believed for so long is not truth; but

---

[2] Note: To those unfamiliar with the original languages, the assistance of commentaries, concordances and an Interlinear will be most helpful.

was that truth acquired in the halls of academia, from the lips of revered pastors or from beloved ancestors? Have you challenged the truth on which you stand? Truth can be found only in Jesus and His Word, the Holy Scriptures.

For example, Matthew 24 has been used by so many to support the teaching of the rapture / harpazo of God's elect. In this teaching, the *great tribulation (v21)* occurs after the rapture / harpazo and those who are not caught up will be left behind on earth to face the ire of the antichrist, the mark of the beast and the wrath of the seven last plagues. In light of this teaching, few have given serious consideration to the flow of the following verses:

> *Matt24:21 for then shall be great tribulation, such as was not since the beginning of the world to this time, no, nor ever shall be. 22 And except those days should be shortened, there should no flesh be saved: but for the elect's sake those days shall be shortened.*

> *Matt24:29 Immediately after the tribulation of those days shall the sun be darkened, and the moon shall not give her light, and the stars shall fall from heaven, and the powers of the heavens shall be shaken: 30 and then shall appear the sign of the Son of man in heaven: and then shall all the tribes of the earth mourn, and they shall see the Son of man coming in the clouds of heaven with power and great glory. 31 And he shall send his angels with a great sound of a trumpet, and they shall gather together his elect from the four winds, from one end of heaven to the other.*

In these verses, the Scripture makes it clear that the tribulation comes first, i.e., before God sends His angels to gather His elect and take them from the earth. This is contrary to the teaching of the rapture / harpazo. Also note the reason why the tribulation is shortened: It is for the elect's sake. The elects are God's people who are going through the tribulation and God shortens the period for their sake.

Other rapture adherents present Matthew 24:40-44 as evidence that some will be snatched away leaving others to gasp at their disappearance:

> *Matt24:40 Then shall two be in the field; the one shall be taken, and the other left. 41 Two women shall be grinding at the mill; the one shall be taken, and the other left. 42 Watch therefore: for ye know not what hour your Lord doth come. 43 But know this, that if the goodman of the house had known in what watch the thief would come, he would have watched, and would not have suffered his house to be broken up. 44 Therefore be ye also ready: for in such an hour as ye think not the Son of man cometh.*

However, note here again, that in the sequence of events outlined in Matthew 24, this event also comes after the tribulation!

Additionally, in Matthew 24, Jesus gives the direst warning to those living in the years after His passion and before his return:

> *Matt24:3 And as he sat upon the mount of Olives, the disciples came unto him privately, saying, Tell us, when shall these things be? and what shall be the sign of thy coming, and of the end of the world?*

His answer:

> *Matt24:4 . . . Take heed that <u>no man deceive you.</u>*

> *Matt24:5 For many shall come in my name, saying, I am Christ; and <u>shall deceive many.</u>*

Matt24:11 *And many false prophets shall rise, and shall deceive many.*

Matt24:24 *For there shall arise false Christs, and false prophets, and shall shew great signs and wonders; insomuch that, if it were possible, they shall deceive the very elect.*

Seven times in this Matthew 24 passage Jesus speaks of deception, false Christs and false teachings that will occur before His return. His clear admonition is to *believe it not (vs: 23, 26).* Remember, the truth is so close to error that, if possible, the very elect shall be deceived.

In the midst of His answer to this tri-part question, Jesus says to His disciples:

Matt2415 *When ye therefore shall see the abomination of desolation, spoken of by Daniel the prophet, stand in the holy place, (whoso readeth, let him understand:)*

Jesus says, if you really want to understand: *when shall these things be? and what shall be the sign of My coming, and of the end of the world?* Study Daniel!

While there is much to unpack in this statement, the takeaway is that of all the books of the Bible, Jesus mentions Daniel in answer to the question about His coming and the end of the world. Jesus also mentions candidly that Daniel is a prophet and not a historian and that Daniel is a recommended study for those who are keenly interested in what the prophecies have to say regarding the events that lead up to the Second Coming and to the end of the world. So, before Matthew 24, or any other portion of Bible prophecies can be fully understood in the correct biblical context, it is recommended by Jesus that a study of the book of

Daniel be undertaken. To this end is the content and purpose of this study.

3: Structures in the writings of Daniel

There is a well-defined structural format in the book of Daniel. However, this is often overlooked by the casual reader. Before the study of the *châzôwn* can be properly undertaken, it will be necessary to have a basic understanding of the format and construction of this apocalyptic work in layman's language. Although we read this book in English with well recognized syntactical punctuation, when first penned these were not present.[3] Additionally, like all other Old Testament works, chapters and verses were not a part of the original construct of this book.[4]

There is also the issue of word usage and meaning. For example, the word "vision" in the English language connotes a variety of meanings. The word 'vision' could have the meaning of a person's sight. It could imply one's personal view of the future or it could mean a divine revelation given by God. The context in which the word is used would be the determinant factor of its meaning. This is not quite so in Aramaic/Hebrew, as in the original language, the word used for vision has a meaning that specifically describes what such a vision entails.

---

[3] "Unlike the versions we read in translation, the Hebrew text contained no punctuation, no commas, quotation marks, upper or lower case, no division between sentences, not even vowels . . . these came into circulation only by the ninth century". Elliot Rabin, *Understanding the Hebrew Bible* (Jersey City, N.J: KTAV Publishing House, Inc., 2006), xiv.

[4] "Chapter and verse division were not marked until the Middle Ages, by Christian scholar Stephen Langton." Ibid.

Without belaboring the point, here are the essentials that must be noted for this study. First, the book of Daniel was written in two languages. The first half is essentially written in Aramaic and the second half is written in Hebrew. In ancient times, these two languages were the bedrock of the Jewish people from their interaction with both the Assyrians and the Babylonians (Chaldeans). There are also some Greek words spattered in the writing. However, without digging deeper, the presence of these Greek words should not presume the dating of the work; but should at the outset be accepted that Greece was a country with a people that were interactive with other people in the then known world.

There is another division contained in the writing of Daniel that must also not be missed. The first half of the writing contains essentially historic data while the second half contains apocalyptic data. So, in the first chapter, Daniel says, "In the third year of the reign of Jehoiakim, king of Judah came Nebuchadnezzar, king of Babylon unto Jerusalem and besieged it" (Dan 1:1). Essentially, Daniel says he was then brought to Babylon as a captive. Chapter 2 recounts, historically, the dream of the Great Metal Man, which King Nebuchadnezzar had along with the interpretation of the same. Chapter 3 tells of the great golden statue that King Nebuchadnezzar built, and of the three Hebrew boys being thrown into the fiery furnace. Chapter 4 tells of Nebuchadnezzar's dream of a tree and his seven-year animalistic ordeal. Chapter 5 details the fateful night that Babylon fell to the Medes and Persians. The final chapter in this historic half is Chapter 6, which speaks of Darius, the Mede setting up his kingdom and Daniel being thrown into the den of lions.

There have been many reasons forwarded as to why the book of Daniel was structured in its present format, which explanations are without end as new data is analyzed; however, such details are not necessary for this study. Chapter 7 of Daniel begins the apocalyptic half of the book with the vision of the Four Great Beasts from the sea. Chapter 8 not only contains the vision of the Ram and the He-goat; but it also begins the Hebrew segment of Daniel. In Chapter 9, Gabriel appears to Daniel and relates to him the prophecy of the Seventy Weeks. Chapter 10 finds Daniel in his final vision, which continues to the end of the book, while the never-ending battles between the king of the North and King of the South are chronicled in Chapter 11. In the final chapter, Michael stands up and there is a time of trouble such as never was, nor shall be. It is at this time that God's people are delivered.

There are those who have noticed that the chapters in the writings of Daniel are not chronologically sequenced. In other words, the first four chapters are chronologically intact. Chapter 5 however, does not follow Chapter 4. Chronologically, both Chapters 7 and 8 follow after Chapter 4. The reason for this observation is simply that Chapter 5 speaks of the end of Belshazzar's reign as this chapter details his death. However, Chapter 7 speaks to events in the first year of his reign and Chapter 8 his third. These two chapters must therefore come before his death. The events of these chapters would therefore obviously also come before his death. Chapters 5 and 6 would therefore follow Chapter 8, with 9 through 12 coming after 6. The full chronology of the writing would then be 1 – 4, 7, 8, 5, 6, 9 – 12.

Another significant observation, particularly regarding the visions of Daniel is to note the construction of each which is evident in all. Each vision has a narrative of the vision itself and a narrative that interprets the vision. These two segments describe the same content. Each vision also ends with a divine component. Using these two construction criteria of the narrative of each vision, it will be subsequently determined how many visionary experiences Daniel had and what they each constitute. Additionally, it will be noted that Daniel uses different Aramaic/Hebrew words to describe each of his visionary experiences. There should then be no discrepancy as to what visionary experiences Daniel had and what was the interpretation given.

Summarily, there should be a general agreement that the book of Daniel contains the story of a young Jewish boy who was taken captive to Babylon, where he remained until his death.[5] The period of his stay in Babylon was from the third year of King Jehoiakim until about the third year of Cyrus the Great, and that the events contained in this writing, were of noted events during this period. These writings contain visions and dreams that have certainly stimulated and intrigued individuals from the times of the writing even to these modern times.

---

[5] Note: See the chapter, "Daniel in the Critics' Den Rebutted" in the study, *Antiochus IV Epiphanes Is Dead,* for the details of this conclusion.

4: *Châzôwn, chălôwm* and *chêzêv*

There is continued debate on every level, from academic scholarship to the layman in the pew as to the number of visions that were given to the prophet Daniel. Some attest as few as three, while others arrive at five. This is an ongoing debate with apparently no place for a consensus. Some will not count the vision of the Great Metal Man in Daniel 2 as a vision that was given to Daniel because the dream was actually first given to King Nebuchadnezzar. Others view the handwriting on the wall of King Belshazzar's palace as a vision because Daniel interpreted it. The debate continues. Without attempting to join this debate, let's approach this dilemma from a different perspective and determine if this longstanding debate can finally be put to rest.

In the English Bibles, the word vision is being used for the many different divine revelations that were received from God; however, in the original languages of the Old Testament, there are several different original words that reflect each of these revelations. Each of these words in the original language connote a unique meaning. Think of it this way. In the English Bibles, the word "vision" is being used as a homograph. One word that carries several different meanings. Therefore, a different approach that might be used to find consensus on the number of visions given to Daniel would be to base this quest on the many different words Daniel used for "vision".

The first recorded use of the word for vision used in Daniel is ch1:17.

*Dan1:17*As for these four children, God gave them knowledge and skill in all learning and wisdom: and Daniel had understanding in all visions and dreams.

The Hebrew word Daniel uses here for visions is חָזוֹן, *châzôwn*[6]. The primary meaning of this word is: vision (in ecstatic state). In the context here in ch1:17. Daniel is letting his readers know that God had given him the gift of understanding these special divine revelations. By denoting "visions and dreams" Daniel further differentiates this means of divine revelation from others. The Aramaic word used here for dreams is: חֲלוֹם, *chălôwm*[7] with a contextual meaning: dream (with prophetic meaning). In this ch1:17 passage, Daniel does not record a vision or a dream; but notes that he does have the unique gift of interpreting both of these.

In Daniel Chapter 2, the familiar story of King Nebuchadnezzar's dream of a great statue is found. Here Daniel differentiates between the subsequent experience he had and that which was given to Nebuchadnezzar. Daniel states that the king dreamed dreams. In speaking of this dream, Daniel not only uses *chălôwm*; but also, a variation of the same root word, חֵלֶם, *chêlem*.[8] Both words carry the same meaning:

---

[6] חָזוֹן, châzôwn, khaw-zone'; from H2372; a sight (mentally), i.e., a dream, revelation, or oracle:—vision. Strong's Concordance with Hebrew and Greek Lexicon, accessed July, 15, 2020, https://www. blueletterbible.org/ lang/Lexicon/ Lexicon.cfm?strongs=H2377&t=KJV

[7] חֲלוֹם, chălôwm, khal-ome'; or (shortened) חֲלֹם chălôm; from H2492; a dream:—dream(-er). Ibid, accessed July, 15, 2020, https://www.blueletterbible. org/lang/Lexicon/Lexicon.cfm?strongs=H2472&t=KJV

*Dan2:1 And in the second year of the reign of
Nebuchadnezzar Nebuchadnezzar dreamed dreams,
wherewith his spirit was troubled, and his sleep brake from
him . . .*

Note carefully that Daniel did not record that the king had a
vision. The words Daniel uses in this portion of the biblical
narrative is essential in understanding the different experiences that
are being described. Here in Daniel Chapter 2, Nebuchadnezzar
had a dream. King Nebuchadnezzar then relates to his magicians
that he had this dream. He had gone to bed and while there he had
a dream, which although he had forgotten, Daniel was able,
subsequently, to relate it to him the very dream, which he had had:

*Dan2:31 Thou, O king, sawest, and behold a great image.
This great image, whose brightness was excellent, stood
before thee; and the form thereof was terrible. 32 This
image's head was of fine gold, his breast and his arms of
silver, his belly and his thighs of brass, 33 his legs of iron,
his feet part of iron and part of clay. 34 Thou sawest till that
a stone was cut out without hands, which smote the image
upon his feet that were of iron and clay, and brake them to
pieces. 35 Then was the iron, the clay, the brass, the silver,
and the gold, broken to pieces together, and became like
the chaff of the summer threshingfloors; and the wind
carried them away, that no place was found for them: and*

---

[8] Note: The Aramaic words chălôwm and חֵלֶם chêlem, H2493 are used
throughout Chapter 2 when referencing Nebuchadnezzar's experience, i.e., 2:1,
2:2. 2:3, 2:4, 2:5, 2:6, 2:7, 2:9, 2:26, 2:28, 2:36, 2:45. Both words are from the
same Aramaic root word, H2492 and carries the same connotation. It is also
used throughout Chapter 4 and in 5:12 and 7:1.

the stone that smote the image became a great mountain, and filled the whole earth.

This was the dream that Nebuchadnezzar had. However, because his magicians were not able to make known to the king the dream and its interpretation, the king had ordered that they all should be put to death. Daniel then requested time and after praying with his friends to God that He would have mercy on them and not allow them to perish along with the wise men of Babylon, he and his friends went to bed and to sleep:

> *Dan2:19* *Then was the secret revealed unto Daniel in a night vision.*

Daniel clearly states that while the king had a *chălôwm*, he, Daniel had a חֱזֵו, *chêzêv.*[9] This Aramaic word means: (vision, appearance). Since both men saw the same great statue, why did Daniel use different Aramaic words to describe their individual encounter? The difference is found in the narrative of each man's experience. God not only showed Daniel the very same image that was shown to King Nebuchadnezzar; but God also gave Daniel the divine revelation associated with this image. So, while the king was given a *chălôwm/chêlem*, a dream that carries a prophetic meaning; however, this divine meaning was not given to the king. Daniel, on the other hand was given a *chêzêv*, which is a dream along with its divine meaning. Daniel then tells the king:

> *Dan2:28* . . . *there is a God in heaven that revealeth secrets, and maketh known to the king Nebuchadnezzar what shall*

---

[9] חֱזֵו chêzêv khay'-zev; (Aramaic) from H2370; a sight:—look, vision. Strong's Concordance with Hebrew and Greek Lexicon, accessed July, 15,2020, https://www.blueletterbible.org/lang/Lexicon/Lexicon.cfm?strongs= H2376&t= KJV.

be in the latter days. Thy dream, and the visions of thy head upon thy bed, are these . . .

Note here that Daniel now speaks to the king of the dream/*chălôwm* and the visions/*chêzêv*.

This usage of these two different words not only reinforces the demarcation of the Aramaic words used for dreams and visions; but it also reflects the combination of Nebuchadnezzar's experience and that of Daniel's experience. In the experience given to Nebuchadnezzar regarding the great image, he had a dream *(chălôwm/chêlem)*. In the experience given to Daniel regarding the same great image, he had a vision *(chêzêv)*. In his *chêzêv*, Daniel had a divine encounter; however, in documenting this event, Daniel simply states:

> *Dan2:19 Then was the secret revealed unto Daniel in a night vision.*

Although the details of Daniel's divine encounter are not given here, in subsequent chapters, it will become more obvious, the manner of Daniel's divine encounter. The difference here then noted is not just the difference in Aramaic words, but a difference in experience. Here we should then agree that while Nebuchadnezzar had a dream, Daniel had a vision. His first!

The next recorded use of the word "vision" is found in Daniel Chapter 4. Here the words of Nebuchadnezzar are recorded:

> *Dan4:4 I Nebuchadnezzar was at rest in mine house, and flourishing in my palace: ⁵ I saw a dream which made me afraid, and the thoughts upon my bed and the visions of my head troubled me.*

Here again, as in Daniel 2:28 the same two English words are found once again, dream (*chêlem*)[10] and visions (*chêzêv*)[11]; however, this time it is recorded that it was Nebuchadnezzar who had both! He has also remembered this dream/vision of a tree that reached up to heaven. Nebuchadnezzar was able to relate to his magicians and also to Daniel the content of what he had dreamt. And although his magicians were not able to provide an interpretation; when called, Daniel was able to provide such. When relating his experience to Daniel, the king clearly states:

> *Dan4:13 I saw in the visions of my head upon my bed, and, behold, a watcher and an holy one came down from heaven;*

In this *chêzêv*, it is Nebuchadnezzar who had a divine encounter. Neither this dream nor vision was given to Daniel, instead, it was told to Daniel by the king. Now while Daniel was standing there, astonished for an hour, and his thoughts troubled him, the king made a most remarkable statement:

> *Dan4:19 . . . The king spake, and said, Belteshazzar, let not the dream, or the interpretation thereof, trouble thee.*

One could almost venture to believe that Nebuchadnezzar had some inclination that this was about himself; but wanted confirmation. Nevertheless, everything that was needed to understand the dream/vision had been given to Nebuchadnezzar. He had had a dream and a divine encounter while asleep. Daniel,

---

[10] Note: This Aramaic word, chêlem, a variation of chălôwm is used throughout Chapter 4 when referencing Nebuchadnezzar's experience, i.e., 4:5, 4:6, 4:7, 4:8, 4:9, 4:18, 4:19.

[11] Note: This Aramaic word, chêzêv, is used throughout Chapter 4 when referencing Nebuchadnezzar's experience, i.e., 4:5, 4:9, 4:10, 4:13.

after giving it some thought, only added that it was about the king. The takeaway from Chapter 4 is that this vision/*chêzêv* was not given to Daniel, but to Nebuchadnezzar.

Daniel Chapter 5 recounts the last night of King Belshazzar's reign. Although there are some scholarly discrepancies as to how long Belshazzar reigned, Daniel 5 states that the fall of Babylon was in the third year of Belshazzar's reign and on that night when he was slain, Darius, the Mede took the kingdom. It was on that fateful night that Belshazzar had seen a hand write upon the plaster of the wall of the king's palace, MENE, MENE, TEKEL, UPHARSIN. Regarding this event, the only reference to dreams/*chêlem* is this:

> *Dan5:12* *Forasmuch as an excellent spirit, and knowledge, and understanding, interpreting of dreams, and shewing of hard sentences, and dissolving of doubts, were found in the same Daniel, whom the king named Belteshazzar: now let Daniel be called, and he will shew the interpretation.*

Here it is the queen who counsels the king to call for Daniel in whom is the spirit of the holy gods and provides the above character reference regarding Daniel. Here again, no vision or dream is recorded.

Since the words vision or dream are not recorded in Daniel Chapter 6, the study moves to Daniel 7. In Daniel Chapter 7, can be found the same two English words dream and vision once again coupled together:

Dan7:1 In the first year of Belshazzar, king of Babylon Daniel had a dream[12] and visions[13] of his head upon his bed: then he wrote the dream, and told the sum of the matters. ²Daniel spake and said, I saw in my vision by night, and, behold, the four winds of the heaven strove upon the great sea.

This narrative paints a picture of Daniel asleep upon his bed and being given a dream along with a divine encounter within that dream. The dream spans verses 2 – 14. It mentions four grotesque beasts, diverse one from another coming up out of the great sea. The divine encounter / exposé begins in ch7:15, which mentions four earthly kingdoms and speaks of the kingdom of God at the end of these earthly kingdoms.

Here, while in the dream, Daniel has an encounter with a divine being. Daniel's dream *(chêlem)* has now become a vision *(chêzêv)*. After asking for the meaning of what he had seen, the angel gives Daniel a summary of this dream:

Dan7:17 These great beasts, which are four, are four kings, which shall arise out of the earth. ¹⁸ But the saints of the most High shall take the kingdom, and possess the kingdom for ever, even for ever and ever.

This succinct response given to Daniel states that there would be four successive kings/kingdoms from the time of the first beast/kingdom until God sets up His kingdom on earth.

---

[12] Note: This Aramaic word, chêlem, in Daniel 7:1 references the entire narrative which is a reference of Daniel's experience

[13] Note: This Aramaic word, chêzêv, is used throughout Chapter 7 when referencing Daniel's experience, i.e., 7:1, 7:2, 7:7; 7:13, 7:15.

Daniel then entered into an elongated conversation with the divine being regarding the dream and was given answers to his many concerns. These are highlighted here in order to demonstrate the connectedness of all of Daniel's divine encounters. One of Daniel's questions was regarding the fourth beast, and he was told that:

> *Dan7:23 . . . The fourth beast shall be the fourth kingdom upon earth, which shall be diverse from all kingdoms, and shall devour the whole earth, and shall tread it down, and break it in pieces.*

Note here that the discussion of this fourth beast is an interpretation of one of the four beasts/kings of ch7:17; but, is here referred to as the fourth kingdom. Kings and kingdoms are here used interchangeably. It must therefore be concluded that at the end of these four earthly kingdoms/empires the kingdom of God will be established on the earth. Sequentially, there is the kingdom of the lion, with eagle's wings, the bear raised up on one side with three ribs in his mouth, the leopard with four wings of a fowl. The fourth was a great and terrible beast with ten horns. From among these ten horns a little horn arose, uprooting three of the previous horns.

Daniel then became focused on this little horn and was told that:

> *Dan7:24 . . . the ten horns out of this kingdom are ten kings that shall arise: and another shall rise after them; and he shall be diverse from the first, and he shall subdue three kings. 25 And he shall speak great words against the most High, and shall wear out the saints of the most High, and think to change times and laws: and they shall be given into his hand until a time and times and the dividing of*

time. [26] But the judgment shall sit, and they shall take away his dominion, to consume and to destroy it unto the end.

Because the Little Horn has been one of the most controverted subjects in Christianity, two points will be mentioned here.[14] (1) Verses 23 – 26 makes it plain that this Little Horn of Chapter 7 is a part of the fourth beast/kingdom and not a beast/kingdom in itself, as the prophecy does not speak about five earthly kingdoms, but four. Therefore, this Little Horn MUST be connected with the fourth kingdom. (2) Verses 20 – 23 states that whenever the Little Horn comes to power, he remains until the coming of the Lord. Thus, the vision states that the Little Horn is present at the judgment as it is at that time that the kingdom is taken from him and given to the saints of the most High:

> *Dan7:26 But the judgment shall sit, and they shall take away his dominion, to consume and to destroy it unto the end. 27 And the kingdom and dominion, and the greatness of the kingdom under the whole heaven, shall be given to the people of the saints of the most High, whose kingdom is an everlasting kingdom, and all dominions shall serve and obey him.*

Like the vision in Daniel 2, which ended with a Rock cut out of the mountain without hands, this vision narrative also ends with a divine component, the judgment. In Daniel 2 there were also four kingdoms:

> *Dan2:40 the fourth kingdom . . . 41 the kingdom shall be divided . . .*

---

[14] Note: For a full study of the little horn, kindly reference the systematic study entitled, *Daniel's Little Horn.*

Both the *chêzêv* of Daniel 2 and 7 convey the same information. They speak of four kingdoms that will span earth's history until the coming kingdom of God. Scholars agree that both the head of the Great Metal Man and the Lion with eagle's wings are fit representations of the kingdom of Babylon.[15] In these visions, recorded in Daniel, there will therefore be a lineage of four earthly kingdoms, i.e., world empires which will continue successively from the time of Babylon until the coming of the Lord. The fourth kingdom will be divided and from which a little horn will emerge. This little horn will then remain until the judgment. This *chêzêv* in Chapter 7 would now be Daniel's second vision / divine encounter.

---

[15] "The first kingdom is identified as Babylon (2: 38), the head of gold (v. 32) and winged lion (7: 4)". Walter C. Kaiser Jr., Garrett, Duane. *NIV, Archaeological Study Bible*, eBook (Kindle Locations 75135-75139). Zondervan. Kindle Edition.

5: The *Châzôwn*

At the outset of the Hebrew portion of his writing, the prophet Daniel writes:

> *Dan8:1 In the third year of the reign of King Belshazzar a vision appeared unto me, even unto me Daniel, after that which appeared unto me at the first. 2 And I saw in a vision; and it came to pass, when I saw, that I was at Shushan in the palace, which is in the province of Elam; and I saw in a vision, and I was by the river of Ulai.*

In this passage of Daniel Chapter 8 there are several changes that occur in the writings of Daniel that will have a profound and definite impact on the rest of the book. To those familiar with the original writings, the first is that there is an obvious change of language from Imperial Aramaic to Hebrew. The second, not so obvious to those unfamiliar with the original language is that the words Daniel uses for vision from here to the end of the book have also been changed. Therefore, going forward, the original words for "vision" will be substituted in the text so as to properly distinguish these original words that are being used and more importantly to effect clarity of content.

These verses in Daniel Chapter 8:1-2 would therefore read as follows:

> *Dan8:1 In the third year of the reign of King Belshazzar a châzôwn appeared unto me, even unto me Daniel, after that which appeared unto me at the first. 2 And I saw in a châzôwn; and it came to pass, when I saw, that I was at*

Shushan in the palace, which is in the province of Elam; and I saw in a châzôwn, and I was by the river of Ulai.

The primary word *chêzêv* that had been used for vision has been changed to *châzôwn*.[16] The reason Daniel uses *châzôwn*, a different word for "vision" in this passage, can be denoted from this visionary experience which he now has. In his previous experiences in chapters two and seven, Daniel had gone to his bed and while he laid there asleep upon his bed, God had given him *chălôwm/chêlem* and *chêzêv*. As have been noted, *chêzêv* is used when there is a dream and a divine encounter within that dream. While a *chălôwm/chêlem* does have a prophetic meaning, the meaning/interpretation is not given in the *chălôwm/chêlem*.

Here in Chapter 8, however, Daniel is not on his bed; but is in an ecstatic state. In this quasi awake state, there are images that he sees as though they are in midair.[17] Daniel is in a *châzôwn* (in ecstatic state). While in this state, he sees images, hears and participates in conversation with divine beings and encounters emotional experiences. The reason for a change of word is therefore not a casual change because of a change of language, but it is a change of experience.

---

[16] Note: The Hebrew word châzôwn is used throughout Chapter 8: 8:1, 8:2, 8:13, 8:15, 8:17, and 8:26, except for the use of mar'eh in 8:15, 8:16, 8:26 and 8:27.

[17] Note: Some have presented arguments to question whether Daniel was physically at the location mentioned in the châzôwn or was at another place. This study will show that it is more reasonable to accept that Daniel was at the location which he mentioned; however, the point here to be concerned with is that Daniel had a markedly different visionary experience, which he noted as a châzôwn meaning he was not asleep and therefore was awake.

There is another Hebrew word that must also be mentioned at this time. This word, מַרְאָה, *mar'eh*[18] interpreted as vision can also be found in this chapter as well as in other chapters throughout the writings of Daniel. Contextually, *mar'eh* is a reference to something that is seen with the naked eye. It is not used in the context of a divine revelation. The word refers to that which is actually seen. It can also mean the physical appearance or countenance of someone.[19] One final word that is used for "vision" in the Hebrew portion of the writing is מַרְאָה, *mar'âh.*[20] Although m*ar'âh* does carry the connotation of a divine revelation, such a revelation is describably different from that of *chêzêv* and *châzôwn.* This will be further looked at in Daniel 10. It is the only place in Daniel's writing where m*ar'âh* is used.

The narrative of the *châzôwn* itself spans Daniel Chapter 8: 1–14. However, as will be shown in this study, the exposé given is found not only in the rest of Chapter 8, but in the rest of the book! One of the most compelling pieces of evidence for this conclusion

---

[18] מַרְאָה, mar'eh, mar-eh'; from H7200; a view (the act of seeing); also an appearance (the thing seen), whether (real) a shape (especially if handsome, comeliness; often plural the looks), or (mental) a vision: - apparently, appearance(-reth), - as soon as beautiful(-ly), countenance, fair, favoured, form, goodly, to look (up) on (to), look(-eth), pattern, to see, seem, sight, visage, vision. Strong's Concordance with Hebrew and Greek Lexicon, accessed July, 15, 2020, https://www.blueletterbible.org/lang/Lexicon/Lexicon.cfm?strongs= H4758&t=KJV.

[19] Note: In Daniel 1:13 and 1:15 it carries the meaning of countenance and in 8:15, 10:6 and 10:18 it means appearance. Something discerned by the naked eye.

[20] מַרְאָה, mar'âh, mar-aw'; feminine of H4759; a vision; also (causatively) a mirror:—looking glass, vision. Ibid, accessed July, 15, 2020, https://www.blueletter bible.org/lang/Lexicon/Lexicon.cfm?strongs =H4759&t=KJV.

is that it is this *châzôwn* that both Gabriel and Daniel continue to explicitly and implicitly reference subsequently in the rest of the book of Daniel. These references are:

Dan8:15 *And it came to pass, when I, even I Daniel, had seen the châzôwn, and sought for the meaning, then, behold, there stood before me as the appearance of a man.*

Dan8:17 *. . . Understand, O son of man: for at the time of the end shall be the châzôwn.*

Dan8:26 *. . . wherefore shut thou up the châzôwn; for it shall be for many days.*

Dan9:21 *yea, whiles I was speaking in prayer, even the man Gabriel, whom I had seen in the châzôwn at the beginning, being caused to fly swiftly, touched me about the time of the evening oblation.*

Dan9:24 *Seventy weeks are determined upon thy people and upon thy holy city . . . to seal up the châzôwn and prophecy*

Dan10:14 *Now I am come to make thee understand what shall befall thy people in the latter days: for yet the châzôwn is for many days.*

Dan11:14 *And in those times there shall many stand up against the king of the south: also the robbers of thy people shall exalt themselves to establish the châzôwn; but they shall fall.*

Dan12:4 *But thou, O Daniel, shut up the words, [of the châzôwn] and seal the book, even to the time of the end: many shall run to and fro, and knowledge shall be increased.*

Dan12:9 And he said, Go thy way, Daniel: for the words [of the châzôwn] are closed up and sealed till the time of the end.

In these preceding verses, as can be seen, it is the *châzôwn* that is consistently mentioned across the remaining chapters in the book of Daniel.

Another compelling reason this study will offer for the *châzôwn* to constitute the subsequent portion of Daniel is that it is the portion of Daniel written exclusively in Hebrew. In other words, in the original writing, Daniel 8:1-12:13 is the portion of Daniel written entirely in Hebrew, while the other chapters are written primarily in Imperial Aramaic. The entire portion, 8:1-12:13 constitutes the *châzôwn* and its exposition. It is a book within a book. Daniel was given direct instructions to *shut thou up the châzôwn . . .* and, *the words [of the châzôwn] are closed up and sealed till the time of the end.* (Daniel 8:26 & 12:9). From Daniel's perspective, having been given this directive, there would be only one of two ways to accomplish this task, either tell no one or to write it in such a way that it is not easily understood. Daniel chose the latter and wrote the *châzôwn* in Hebrew.

While Imperial Aramaic was the de facto universal language of the day, Hebrew was spoken only amongst the Jews, and they were scattered across the Assyrian and Babylonian territories. Additionally, since Daniel, by Jewish standards was not considered to be a prophet, his writings therefore would not be a part of the Nevi'im ('Prophets') section of the Tanakh; but instead, it became a part of the Ketuvim ('Writings') section in the Hebrew Bible. Since it was not a part of the Nevi'im ('Prophets') portion of the Tanakh these prophetic words of the *châzôwn* pertaining to the latter days would be locked away for a very long time.

A third reason offered for the *châzôwn* to constitute the remaining portions of Daniel is that subsequent to the voice telling Gabriel to make Daniel understand what he had seen, Gabriel continues to use the word "understand" in reference to the *châzôwn:*

> *Dan8:16 And I heard a man's voice between the banks of Ulai, which called, and said, Gabriel, make this man to* understand *the mar'eh [i.e., understand what you have seen].* [17] *... he said unto me,* Understand, *O son of man: for at the time of the end shall be the châzôwn.*

> *Dan9:23 At the beginning of thy supplications the commandment came forth, and I am come to shew thee; for thou art greatly beloved: therefore* understand *the matter, and consider the mar'eh [i.e. consider what you have seen].* [24] *Seventy weeks are determined upon thy people and upon thy holy city ... to seal up the châzôwn and prophecy, and to anoint the most Holy.* [25] *Know therefore and* understand, *that, from the going forth of the commandment to restore and to build Jerusalem unto the Messiah[21] the Prince shall be seven weeks, and threescore and two weeks:*

> *Dan 10:11 And he said unto me, O Daniel, a man greatly beloved,* understand *the words that I speak unto thee, and stand upright: for unto thee am I now sent.*

---

[21] Note: It has been generally accepted that the "Messiah" here mentioned in Daniel 9, i.e., "the anointed One" is a reference to Christ. See Acts 10:37, 38.

Dan10:14 *Now I am come to make thee <u>understand</u> what shall befall thy people in the latter days: for yet the châzôwn is for many days*

Having been commissioned to *make Daniel understand,* Gabriel continues to use the very word in subsequent conversations.

Note very carefully that in ch8:16 the voice tells Gabriel to make Daniel understand the *mar'eh;* however, when Gabriel comes to Daniel in ch8:17, he speaks to Daniel of the *châzôwn* telling him to understand that the *châzôwn* shall be at the time of the end. The same occurrence can be found in ch9:23 & 24 where Gabriel tells Daniel to understand the *mar'eh;* but then tells Daniel that seventy weeks will seal up the *châzôwn.*

In ch9:25 he speaks to Daniel regarding the start of the seventy weeks prophecy, which will be shown to be coincident with the start of the *châzôwn.* In Chapter 10 Daniel is again told to understand the *châzôwn.* As pointed out earlier in this chapter of study, *mar'eh* acts like a pointer. It is "the thing that is seen". Daniel 8:1, 2 specifically states that Daniel had a *châzôwn.* He did not have a *mar'eh.* Throughout Chapter 8, whenever *mar'eh* is translated as vision, it always points to the *châzôwn* and never to itself. It is the many aspects of the *châzôwn,* throughout the rest of the narrative that Gabriel continues to cause Daniel to understand.

A final reason for the *châzôwn* and its subsequent interpretations to constitute the narrative of Daniel Chapters 8 – 12 is that there are questions asked at the outset of the *châzôwn* in Chapter 8 by the two heavenly beings, for which no answer is provided until Chapter 12 and in the narrative regarding this conversation, the scene is the same and the words tie what was said then in Chapter 12 to what was said earlier in Chapter 8. These two similar scenes serve as it were, like bookends to the narrative of the *châzôwn*. More on this subsequently.

It was by the river of Ulai, at Shushan, in the palace, where Daniel experienced the *châzôwn*. As will be determined, it is the only *châzôwn* that is recorded in the entire book of Daniel![22] Therefore any reference to the *châzôwn* must be a reference to that which is recorded in Daniel 8:1-14. In the *châzôwn*, Daniel sees a ram with two horns; a he-goat with a notable horn; there is a little horn,[23] which waxed exceeding great, toward the south, east, and pleasant *land*; and there is also a conversation between two saints, regarding a time element and the sanctuary. These are the four items[24] of Daniel's awareness in this *châzôwn*. When Daniel sought for a meaning, Gabriel was sent to make him understand:

> *Dan8:16 And I heard a man's voice between the banks of Ulai, which called, and said, Gabriel, make this man to understand the mar'eh [i.e., understand what you have seen]. 17 So he came near where I stood: and when he came, I was afraid, and fell upon my face: but he said unto*

---

[22] Note: Other prophets such as Isaiah, Isa. 1:1; Jerimiah, Jer. 14:14 and Ezekiel, Eze. 7:13, 26, etc. also mention this method of divine revelation.

[23] Note: In Daniel Chapter 7, a little horn emerges following the ten horns that is connected to the fourth beast, and is therefore a component of the fourth kingdom/empire, i.e., the non-descript beast. In Daniel Chapter 8, a little horn is seen subsequent to the he-goat. Most modern critical commentaries see this difference as indicating that this little horn of Chapter 8 as being a component of the he-goat and being the person of Antiochus IV Epiphanes. For a full discussion of the difference and similarities of these two little horns, please see the systematic study, *The Visions of Daniel.*

[24] Note: For this study, the conversation, although containing multiple elements, is counted as one item, i.e., it is one conversation.

*me, Understand, O son of man: for at the time of the
end shall be the châzôwn.*

The Hebrew word for "vision" used by the man's voice when
instructing Gabriel is *mar'eh*. [25] However, when Gabriel spoke to
Daniel, he used the word *châzôwn*. Since these are the two
primary words used for "vision" throughout the rest of the book of
Daniel, it will be necessary to develop a working understanding of
the difference between these two Hebrew words, *châzôwn* and
mar'eh.

Whenever *châzôwn* is used, it embodies the
vision/visionary experience itself and when *mar'eh* is used it is to
refer to the visionary experience of the prophet. The following
verses reflect every occurrence of *mar'eh* that is used for "vision"
in Chapter 8. Verse 26 also provides a good example of how these
two words function together in a sentence. Accordingly, the
English words in these verses have been transposed to the
corresponding Hebrew words:

> *Dan8:16 And I heard a man's voice between the banks
> of Ulai, which called, and said, Gabriel, make this man to
> understand the mar'eh.*

> *Dan8:26 And the mar'eh of the evening and the morning
> which was told is true: wherefore shut thou up the
> châzôwn; for it shall be for many days.*

---

[25] Note: The underlying Greek of Luke 1:19 identifies Gabriel as one
that stands in the very presence of God. The meaning thereby connoted is that
the One who here and in 12:6 gives direction to this mighty angel is God / Son
of God as in Dan. 3:25.

Dan8:27 *And I Daniel fainted, and was sick certain days; afterward I rose up, and did the king's business; and I was astonished at the mar'eh, but none understood it.*

What must be clearly understood is that *mar'eh* DOES NOT constitute either a new vision or a vision of itself. *Mar'eh* should also not be equated with *châzôwn*. While, in the English language, both words are translated as "vision", in the original language they connote two very different meanings. To cement this concept, the following verse is offered:

Dan8:15 *And it came to pass, when I, even I Daniel, had seen the châzôwn, and sought for the meaning, then, behold, there stood before me as the mar'eh of a man.*

The *"mar'eh"* that Daniel saw in Daniel 8, would be the *mar'eh* of a man, i.e., the appearance of a man. If the word *mar'eh* connoted a visionary experience, then when the voice had instructed Gabriel to make Daniel understand the *mar'eh*, the interpretation that should then have followed should have been regarding the *mar'eh* of the man that was between the banks of the River Ulai. However, that which Gabriel presented was the interpretation of the *châzôwn*.

Having been commissioned to make Daniel understand, as had been done by the angel in Chapter 7 with the vision of the Four Great Beasts from the sea, Gabriel first provides Daniel with a succinct overview of the *châzôwn:*

Dan8:17 *So he came near where I stood: and when he came, I was afraid, and fell upon my face: but he said unto me, Understand, O son of man: for at the time of the end shall be the châzôwn.*

Here must be noted a phrase, *"the time of the end"* that is found only in the book of Daniel and only in the *châzôwn* and its subsequent interpretation. Gabriel tells Daniel that this *châzôwn* has something to do with *"the time of the end"*. It is this *châzôwn* and NOT the *mar'eh* that is to be sealed / shut up until *"the time of the end"* (Dan 8:26). A pertinent question that must be answered is, when is *the time of the end* and what does it have to do with the *châzôwn*? This will be unpacked subsequently in this study.

For now, Gabriel proceeds to provide the *understanding* of the elements of the *châzôwn*, which Daniel had seen:

> *Dan8:20 The ram which thou sawest having two horns are the kings of Media and Persia. 21 And the rough goat is the king of Grecia: and the great horn that is between his eyes is the first king. 22 Now that being broken, whereas four stood up for it, four kingdoms shall stand up out of the nation, but not in his power. 23 And in the latter time of their kingdom, when the transgressors are come to the full, a king of fierce countenance, and understanding dark sentences, shall stand up.*

Note the following direct correlation of the *châzôwn* to its interpretation: the ram symbolizes all the kings of Media and Persia.[26] The he-goat represents all the kings of Grecia. The little horn is the king/kingdom of fierce countenance that would stand up in the latter time of these four kingdoms. This little horn would come into existence after the Grecian Empire would be broken up

---

[26] Note: Some have asserted that Media and Persia are two separate kingdoms by virtue of the two horns and should therefore constitute two distinguishable kingdoms. While this may be true, the *châzôwn*, denoted both Media and Persia in the symbol of the ram as one kingdom/empire, i.e., one ram represents all the kings of Media and Persia.

and subsequently subdivided into its four Hellenistic Kingdoms. It is not until the latter times of these four Hellenistic Kingdoms that this little horn kingdom would then come to power, not before![27]

It was also mentioned in the conversation portion of the *châzôwn*:

> *Dan8:14* . . . *Unto two thousand and three hundred days; then shall the sanctuary be cleansed.*

Whatever this sanctuary is and wherever it is located, it would be cleansed sometime after these two thousand and three hundred days would have expired; however, nothing in the interpretive section of Chapter 8 was said to Daniel regarding this conversation nor the time component of the *châzôwn* nor of this sanctuary! The narrative provides a clear reason for this:

> *Dan8:27* *And I Daniel fainted, and was sick certain days; afterward I rose up, and did the king's business; and I was astonished at the mar'eh, [that which was seen] but none understood it.*

There is a factual position that must be asserted at this point in the study. After having heard the interpretation given by Gabriel, Daniel states that he does not understand it. Whether this means the entire vision or a portion of it is for us to now examine.

There are two chapters in Daniel that make explicit reference to this third year of Belshazzar's reign. These are Chapters 5 and 8. This study has already shown that the chapters in the book of Daniel are not chronologically sequenced.

---

[27] Note: Syria and Egypt became part of the Roman Empire in 64bc and 30bc respectively.

Although Chapter 5 is recorded before Chapter 8, it must be reckoned chronologically after Chapter 8. Here is the empirical reason. In Chapter 5 Belshazzar dies. The timing of Belshazzar's death is coincident with the fall of Babylon, historically reckoned as October 539bc. In that night:

> *Dan5:1 Belshazzar the king made a great feast to a thousand of his lords, and drank wine before the thousand . . . 5 In the same hour came forth fingers of a man's hand, and wrote over against the candlestick upon the plaister of the wall of the king's palace: and the king saw the part of the hand that wrote . . . 25 And this is the writing that was written, MENE, MENE, TEKEL, UPHARSIN*

Note Daniel's interpretation of one of these words:

> *Dan5:28 PERES; Thy kingdom is divided, and given to the Medes and Persians. 28*

Here Belshazzar is told that the Babylonian Empire will end and that the Medes and Persian Empire will begin.

Although Daniel had had two previous *chêzêvs* and had been told that Babylon was the first kingdom, he had not been factually told of any other kingdom(s) by name that would be part of the interpretation of the *chêzêvs*. Daniel only knew that there would be four earthly kingdoms that would constitute the prophetic lineage of empires before the coming kingdom of God. Standing there before King Belshazzar and interpreting the handwriting on

---

[28] Note the difference between upharsin and peres. Peres means "share," or "portion," and if the plural form *upharsin* (v. 25) is adopted, may be translated, "pieces."

the wall, Daniel is now able to tell the king that which had already been revealed to him. Daniel would only have been able to do this because the *châzôwn* must therefore have occurred prior to the handwriting on the wall. Daniel must have already been shown that the next kingdom, represented by the ram is Media Persia, and that the he-goat represents Grecia. Having received the *châzôwn* prior to the handwriting on the wall, Daniel would then have been able to relate to Belshazzar that the kingdom by name which would immediately succeed Babylon would be Media Persia.

Having understood that Babylon constituted the first kingdom in the prophetic lineage and subsequently that Media Persia being the second and Grecia the third, Daniel would now understand that there would be one kingdom, a fourth, which would extend from the days following the third kingdom, Greece unto the kingdom of God. As represented in the feet and toes of the Great Metal Man and the head of the non-descript beast of the Four Great Beasts from the sea, this fourth kingdom would be a divided kingdom. It should not be difficult to now conclude that Daniel understood some portions; but not all of the *châzôwn*. Obviously, that which Daniel did not understand was the conversation regarding the time element associated with the sanctuary, as Gabriel, although commissioned to make Daniel understand, provided no interpretation regarding the conversation that had to do with this time element[29] and the sanctuary. Obviously, because Daniel had fainted.

---

[29] Note: Some have asserted that Daniel 8:9-14 and 23-25 reflects events which transpired during the Maccabean period and the reign of Antiochus IV Epiphanes. For a full composition of these points, see the systematic study entitled, *Antiochus IV Epiphanes is Dead.*

Another peculiarity that must be noted is that Daniel was told to shut up the *châzôwn* for it shall be for many days:

> *Dan8:26* *And the mar'eh [that which you have seen] of the evening and the morning which was told is true: wherefore shut thou up the châzôwn; for it shall be for many days.*

How to interpret the *"many days"* has been the subject of many volumes of varied commentaries. As noted, before, there is a direct link between the phrase recorded in the succinct overview of the *châzôwn*, *"at the time of the end shall be the châzôwn,"* and this statement that the *châzôwn* shall be for *"many days"*. Both contain a time factor that cannot yet be addressed in this study, because there has not been enough information given by Gabriel to the full understanding of these. Unless careful study has been given to what exactly constitutes *"the time of the end"* it would be premature to attempt any understanding of what these *"many days"* would refer to. Also note carefully that it was not the entire *châzôwn* that was to be shut up, but that portion that had to do with *"the evening and the morning"*, a phrase first found in conjunction with each day of creation. The implication here is that it is the portion of the *châzôwn*, the conversation that had to do with time that was to be shut up, *for it shall be for many days.* Thus by association, the sanctuary, which would be cleansed after the time element had expired, would then be understood.

This *châzôwn* would then constitute the third visionary experience given to the prophet Daniel!

6: A Vital Link . . . Missing

Daniel Chapter 9 opens with Daniel studying the seventy-year prophecy of Jeremiah and praying. In this prayer, in the 1st year of Darius, the Mede, can be found that which is heaviest on Daniel's heart:

> *Dan9:16 O Lord, according to all thy righteousness, I beseech thee, let thine anger and thy fury be turned away from thy city Jerusalem, thy holy mountain: because for our sins, and for the iniquities of our fathers, Jerusalem and thy people are become a reproach to all that are about us. 17 Now therefore, O our God, hear the prayer of thy servant, and his supplications, and cause thy face to shine upon thy sanctuary that is desolate, for the Lord's sake. 18 O my God, incline thine ear, and hear; open thine eyes, and behold our desolations, and the city which is called by thy name: for we do not present our supplications before thee for our righteousnesses, but for thy great mercies. 19 O Lord, hear; O Lord, forgive; O Lord, hearken and do; defer not, for thine own sake, O my God: for thy city and thy people are called by thy name.*

While in captivity, Daniel had ever turned his face towards Jerusalem and the sanctuary, which were both now in ruins and had prayed (Daniel 6:10), as he has done here in this passage, for the restoration of Jerusalem and the sanctuary and the release of his people. But, after experiencing the *châzôwn,* in his attempt to understand the conversation regarding the time element as it relates to the sanctuary, Daniel is studying Jeremiah's seventy-year prophecy. His reason for studying Jeremiah is simply because it was through Jeremiah that God had said Israel would be captive in Babylon for seventy years.[30] In his prayer, here in Chapter 9:19, Daniel begs God to *"defer not"*. Daniel is here asking God not to change His mind regarding this seventy-year prophecy and the release of His people so that the sanctuary in Jerusalem can be restored and God's name exalted. In other words, Daniel is studying the time element as it relates to the restoration of sanctuary at Jerusalem, the very elements that were not explained to him by Gabriel!

A careful study of Daniel's prayer here in Chapter 9 will underscore the mindset of Daniel since his vision of Chapter 8. Of the four elements in the *châzôwn* of Chapter 8, Gabriel had not provided to Daniel any interpretation regarding the time element as it relates to the sanctuary except to say:

Dan8:14 *. . . Unto two thousand and three hundred days; then shall the sanctuary be cleansed.*

In the writings of Daniel, the word "sanctuary" is used six times. Three times in Chapter 8, twice in Chapter 9 and once in Chapter 11. However, there are two different words that are used for "sanctuary", מִקְדָּשׁ, *miqdâsh*[31] and קֹדֶשׁ, *qôdesh.* [32] The basic

---

[30] Jerimiah 25:11, 12; 29:10.

[31] מִקְדָּשׁ, miqdâsh, mik-dawsh'; or מִקְּדָשׁ miqqᵉdâsh; (Exodus 15:17), from H6942; a consecrated thing or place, especially, a palace, sanctuary (whether of Jehovah or of idols) or asylum:—chapel, hallowed part, holy place, sanctuary. Strong's Concordance with Hebrew and Greek Lexicon, accessed July, 15, 2020, https://www. blueletterbible.org/ lang/Lexicon/ Lexicon.cfm? strongs=H4270&t=KJV

[32] קֹדֶשׁ, qôdesh, ko'-desh; from H6942; a sacred place or thing; rarely abstract, sanctity:—consecrated (thing), dedicated (thing), hallowed (thing), holiness, (most) holy (day, portion, thing), saint, sanctuary. Ibid, accessed July,

difference between the two is that *miqdâsh* can also be used to reference a place for idol worship while *qôdesh* cannot. *Miqdâsh* can also be used to reference an earthly deity, while *qôdesh* cannot. *Miqdâsh* is anyone's sanctuary, while *qôdesh* is God's sanctuary. In order to understand which sanctuary will be cleansed at the end of the two thousand three hundred days, it first becomes important to know which word is used for sanctuary in the conversation between the two saints in the *châzôwn* of Chapter 8.

> *Dan8:13* *Then I heard one saint speaking, and another saint said unto that certain saint which spake, How long shall be the vision concerning the daily ~~sacrifice~~, and the transgression of desolation, to give both the qôdesh and the host to be trodden under foot?* ¹⁴ *And he said unto me, Unto two thousand and three hundred days; then shall the qôdesh be cleansed.*[33]

This sanctuary being discussed by the two saints in the *châzôwn* of Chapter 8 is definitely God's sanctuary. We can therefore conclude that at the end of the time period mentioned in the *châzôwn*, God's sanctuary will be cleansed. However, as he continues in his prayer here in ch9:17, when speaking about God's sanctuary at Jerusalem, Daniel uses *miqdâsh;* but in ch9:26, when speaking about the city and the sanctuary being destroyed after the cutting off of Messiah,[34] Gabriel again uses *qôdesh*. Although the

---

19, 2020, https://www. blueletterbible.org/ lang/Lexicon/ Lexicon.cfm? strongs =H4720&t=KJV.

[33] Note: ~~Strikethrough~~ in a word throughout this study signifies its absence in the original biblical text.

[34] Note: See Footnote 21.

historical context does suggest that it is God's sanctuary that is being spoken of in all these references, it would be a rush to judgment at this point in the study to categorically conclude the location of the sanctuary here being discussed by the heavenly beings.[35] The most that can be stated factually about the *qôdesh* and *châzôwn* from Chapter 8 is:

> *Dan8:14* . . . *Unto two thousand and three hundred days; then shall the qôdesh be cleansed.*

> *Dan8:17* . . . Understand, O son of man: for at the time of the end *shall be* the *châzôwn*.

> *Dan8:26* . . . wherefore shut thou up the *châzôwn*; for it *shall be* for many days.

It is evident from the narrative of Chapter 8 and the conversation which he had then with Gabriel that there is something that Daniel does not understand. This can be further evidenced by Daniel's statement at the end of his interaction with Gabriel in the *châzôwn* of Chapter 8. Something is missing! And since that time in the 3rd year of Belshazzar's reign, 539bc until this 1st year of Darius, the Mede[36], 538bc, approximately two years

---

[35] Note: Some have asserted that the sanctuary to be cleansed, referred to in Daniel 8:14, reflects events which transpired during the Maccabean period and the reign of Antiochus IV Epiphanes. For a full composition of these points, see the systematic study entitled, *Antiochus IV Epiphanes is Dead.*

[36] "Cyrus was Darius' co-regent, the hereditary king of the realm of Persia, the crown prince of Media, and the commander of the Medo-Persian army—yet it was still Darius who was officially recognized as the highest power in the realm. Darius died naturally within two years after the fall of Babylon, and as he had no male heir and Cyrus had married his daughter, Cyrus inherited his position upon his death and united the Median and Persian kingdoms in a

in actual time has elapsed, as the Jews use inclusive reckoning in their count of time, Daniel has been searching for such an understanding. From Jeremiah's writings, Daniel understands that the Jews would be in captivity for seventy years. This Daniel now understands is to end in 536bc.[37]   After which they would return to restore Jerusalem and the worship of Yahweh in a rebuilt sanctuary. In Chapter 9, the 1st year of Darius, the Mede, Daniel, himself has now been in captivity since the first wave of Jewish captives were taken from Jerusalem in 605bc. From that time until now, 538bc he has been in Babylonian captivity for some 67 years.[38] The statement that troubles Daniel is that, while in the *châzôwn*, Gabriel had told him that the *qôdesh* would not be cleansed for yet another 2,300 days. The very simplest of calculations, by simply dividing these days by Jewish years, would yield 6.4 years. Beginning from the time of the *châzôwn* in 539bc, this would place the return of the Jews and the restoration of the city and sanctuary somewhere beyond the seventy-year prophetic mark of 536bc, (539-6.4=532.6), which God had spoken by the mouth of the prophet Jeremiah. Daniel therefore begs God to defer not, not to change His mind.

It is here, in the midst of Daniel's supplication and prayer that Gabriel shows up:

---

single throne." Steven D. Anderson, *Darius the Mede: A Reappraisal* (Scots Valley, CA: CreateSpace, 2014), 1.

[37] Note: To calculate 70 years from 605bc: 605-70=535 (with inclusive reckoning, a normal method of the Jewish chronological system, you would need to add 1, bringing the end of the seventy-year captivity to 536bc

[38] Note: For a detailed study of the chronology of this period see the systematic study: *The Visions of Daniel.*

Dan9:20 *And whiles I was speaking, and praying, and*
confessing my sin and the sin of my people Israel, and
presenting my supplication before the LORD *my God for the*
holy mountain of my God; *21* *yea, whiles I was speaking in*
prayer, even the man Gabriel, whom I had seen in the
châzôwn at the beginning, being caused to fly swiftly,
touched me about the time of the evening oblation.

In this reference to Gabriel, Daniel mentions that he had seen
Gabriel before. He recognizes him because he had seen Gabriel
before in the *châzôwn* that is recorded in Chapter 8. It was Gabriel
that the voice at the River Ulai had sent to make Daniel understand
what he had seen in the *châzôwn*. It was Gabriel that had given
Daniel the interpretation of the symbols which Daniel had then
seen. Gabriel now speaks to Daniel:

Dan9:23 *At the beginning of thy supplications the*
commandment came forth, and I am come to shew thee; for
thou art greatly beloved: therefore <u>understand</u> *the matter,*
and consider the mar'eh.

As will be unpacked in the upcoming chapter, Gabriel now
speaks to Daniel's quest for an understanding of the conversation
component regarding the time element and the sanctuary that was
mentioned in the *châzôwn*. This is just what Daniel has been
missing. He had not understood how to compute the time
component mentioned in the *châzôwn* in relation to the *qôdesh*.
That Gabriel had now come to explain this time element is just
what Daniel has been missing.

7: Consider the *Mar'eh*

Look carefully at Gabriel's first words to Daniel as he informs the prophet of the reason for now coming to him:

> *Dan9:22* O Daniel, I am now come forth to give thee skill and <u>understanding</u>. ²³ At the beginning of thy supplications the commandment came forth, and I am come to shew thee; for thou art greatly beloved: therefore <u>understand</u> the matter, and consider the mar'eh.

In order to fulfill the mandate given to him in Chapter 8:17, to make Daniel <u>understand</u> the mar'eh, Gabriel has now returned. He tells Daniel that he is now come to give him skill and understanding. He tells Daniel to understand the matter and to consider the *mar'eh*. The context of Gabriel's statement enables a clear understanding of what is being asked of Daniel. Daniel is to consider what he had observed, i.e., <u>seen and heard,</u> before, in the *châzôwn*.

The phrase, *"consider the mar'eh"* does not denote a new visionary experience as some have presented.[39] As previously noted, whenever the word *mar'eh* is used for "vision"[40] in the writings of Daniel, it refers to something outside of itself and is not a thing of itself. It is the thing that is seen. Consider the following

---

[39] Note: Both Preterism and Futurism erroneously consider this a separate visionary experience with no connection to the *châzôwn* of Dan 8:1-14.

[40] Mar'eh is also used to connote appearance in these references: in Daniel 1:13 and 1:15 it carries the meaning of countenance and in 8:15, 10:6 and 10:18 it means appearance.

usage of all the references that Daniel makes regarding *mar'eh* that's interpreted as "vision":

> *Dan8:16* . . . *Gabriel, make this man to understand the mar'eh.*

> *Dan8:26* *And the mar'eh of the evening and the morning which was told is true:*

> *Dan8:27* . . . *I was astonished at the mar'eh, but none understood it.*

> *Dan9:23* . . . *understand the matter, and consider the mar'eh.*

> *Dan10:1* . . . *he understood the thing, and had understanding of the mar'eh.*

Additionally, the phraseology that Daniel uses when receiving a visionary experience is missing in this encounter with Gabriel. Note the phraseology used by Daniel with regard to the other visionary experiences that he has recorded:

> *Dan2:19* *Then was the secret revealed unto Daniel in a night chêzêv.*

> *Dan4:4* *I Nebuchadnezzar was at rest in mine house, and flourishing in my palace: 5 I saw a dream which made me afraid, and the thoughts upon my bed and the chêzêv of my head troubled me.*

> *Dan7:1* *In the first year of Belshazzar king of Babylon Daniel had a dream and chêzêv of his head upon his bed:*

> *Dan8:1* *In the third year of the reign of King Belshazzar a châzôwn appeared unto me, even unto me Daniel, after that which appeared unto me at the first*

Danq10:7 And I Daniel alone saw the mar'âh: for the men that were with me saw not the mar'âh

Daniel NEVER uses *mar'eh* to convey an actual visionary experience. Consequently, there is no new "vision" recorded in Daniel Chapter 9! This will become even more evident with Daniel's next visionary encounter at the River Hiddekel.

Further to this point, when Gabriel had said to Daniel:

Dan9:23 . . . understand the matter, and consider the mar'eh

He directly connects what he is about to say, with the conversation that had previously occurred between the two saints in the *châzôwn* of Chapter 8. The original word Gabriel uses here in Chapter 9 for *matter* is דָּבָר, *dâbâr*[41], i.e., something spoken. In the *châzôwn* of Chapter 8, Daniel saw some things, *mar'eh,* and he heard some things, *dâbâr.* The *châzôwn* therefore had two components, a visual component and an auditory component. In the visual component, Daniel saw a ram, a he-goat and a little horn. Gabriel had given him an understanding of what these meant. The ram is Media-Persia, the he-goat is Grecia and the little horn is a king of fierce countenance. He had also seen and heard two saints speaking, which Daniel recorded this way:

Dan8:13 Then I heard one saint dâbar, and another saint said unto that certain saint which dâbar, How long shall be the châzôwn concerning the daily sacrifice, and the transgression of desolation, to give both the qôdesh and the host to be trodden under foot? 14 And he said unto me,

---

[41] דָּבָר, dâbâr, daw-baw'; from H1696; a word; by implication, a matter (as spoken of) or thing. Strong's Concordance with Hebrew and Greek Lexicon, accessed Aug, 22, 2020. https://www.blueletter bible.org/lang/Lexicon/Lexicon.cfm?strongs= H1697&t=KJV.

Unto two thousand and three hundred days; then shall the qôdesh be cleansed.

It was this **דָּבָר**, *dâbar*[42] i.e., conversation, regarding the sanctuary and time that Daniel had not understood as Gabriel had not given him an interpretation regarding these! It was for this understanding that Daniel had gone searching for an answer in the writings of Jeremiah. Now on his return to Daniel in Chapter 9, Gabriel says:

Dan9:23 . . . *understand the dâbâr, and consider the mar'eh*

Gabriel plainly said to Daniel, I have come to bring you an understanding of the *dâbâr*, i.e., the conversation which you had observed, in the *châzôwn*. Another way to understand this is to note that in the vision of Daniel 8, there are two components, visual and auditory. The voice had told Gabriel to make Daniel understand the visual components, the *mar'eh*, the things that were shown to him, i.e., the ram, the he-goat and the little horn. These are the things Daniel saw. The auditory components, the conversation between the two heavenly beings were later explained to Daniel in Chapters 9-

Gabriel's next statement makes plain that he is here to make Daniel understand something to do with time and the sanctuary as it relates to the *châzôwn*:

---

[42] **דָּבָר**, dâbar, daw-bar, a primitive root; perhaps properly, to arrange; but used figuratively (of words), to speak; rarely (in a destructive sense) to subdue:—answer, appoint, bid, command, commune, declare, destroy, give, name, promise, pronounce, rehearse, say, speak, be spokesman, subdue, talk, teach, tell, think, use (entreaties), utter, well, work. Strong's Concordance with Hebrew and Greek Lexicon, accessed Aug, 22, 2020. https://www.blueletter bible.org/lang/Lexicon/ Lexicon.cfm?strongs= H1696&t=KJV.

Dan9:24 *Seventy weeks are determined upon thy people and upon thy holy city, to finish the transgression, and to make an end of sins, and to make reconciliation for iniquity, and to bring in everlasting righteousness, and to seal up the châzôwn and prophecy, and to anoint the most Holy.* [43]

While there is a lot to unpack in this statement, this study will only focus on two of the phrases. [44] (1) *"Seventy weeks are determined"*. The primary meaning of the word *determined*, חָתַךְ, *châthak* [45] in the original language is to cut off. Gabriel essentially starts his explanation to Daniel by referencing a time component of seventy weeks, stating that these "seventy weeks are cut off". This cutting off is not actual but figurative; but from what is it to be cut off. The following statement of Gabriel provides the answer. (2) *"Seventy weeks are determined . . . to seal up the châzôwn and prophecy"*. In this statement of Gabriel, the narrative of the seventy weeks of Chapter 9 is indisputably connected to the narrative of the *châzôwn* of Chapter 8!

One identifying characteristic of these seventy weeks is that it seals up the *châzôwn and prophecy*. There is only one *châzôwn* in the entire book of Daniel and it is located in Daniel Chapter 8:1-14. As will be determined, this time component, these seventy weeks are not only cut off from the two thousand and three

---

[43] Note: In Hebrew culture, the reference to "the Most Holy" can only be understood in relation to the sanctuary.

[44] Note: For a detailed study of these seventy-weeks, see the systematic study: *Roots of Evangelical Lies.*

[45] חָתַךְ, châthak, khaw-thak'; a primitive root; properly, to cut off, i.e. (figuratively) to decree:—determine. Strong's Concordance with Hebrew and Greek Lexicon, accessed Dec, 19, 2020, https://www. blueletterbible.org/ lang/ Lexicon/ Lexicon.cfm?strongs=H2852&t=KJV

hundred days of the *châzôwn* of Chapter 8; but these seventy weeks also seals up the *châzôwn and prophecy.*

8: Seal up the Châzôwn and Prophecy

Whatever is one's understanding of the narrative of these seventy weeks of Daniel Chapter 9, one thing is irrefutable, it cannot be separated from the narrative of the *châzôwn* of Chapter 8 as the *châzôwn* is explicitly mentioned in the narrative of Chapter 9 by Gabriel. Several authors have put forth that the 2,300 days are linked to Antiochus IV Epiphanes and the Maccabean period, and that the seventy weeks reach unto the time of Messiah. In other words, the 2300 days terminate prior to the seventy weeks. If this is true, how would the seventy week prophecy then seal up the *châzôwn and prophecy?* To better comprehend Gabriel's statement, it is critical to understand the meaning of the original word used for seal.

> *Dan9:24* *Seventy weeks are determined upon thy people and upon thy holy city . . . and to châtham the châzôwn and prophecy.*

The usage of this word, חָתַם, *châtham*[46] in the original language is as a verb. Verbs are action words, binding two components of a sentence together. Their action is normally with regard to something outside of itself, i.e., the noun or the subject of the sentence and the object. The subject of this verse is the *seventy*

---

[46] חָתַם châtham, khaw-tham'; a primitive root; to close up; especially to seal:—make an end, mark, seal (up), stop. Strong's Concordance with Hebrew and Greek Lexicon, accessed July, 15, 2020, https://www. blueletterbible.org/ lang/Lexicon/ Lexicon.cfm?strongs=H2856&t=KJV.

weeks, the verb is *seal up* and the object is the *châzôwn and prophecy*. Once bound, they cannot evermore be separated.

The two most common applications in the original language for *châtham* is (1) to seal: to affix one's seal. This seal is the unique mark of an entity, individual or corporate that is affixed to a document. Although of vital importance, it is usually the secondary or a sub-component of the document. The document is the most important, while the seal validates or gives credibility and authenticity to the document. The second most common application is (2) to seal up: fasten up by sealing. This application is to ensure that the content of something is not breached, spilt or lost. The content of what is being sealed is secured by the sealing agent. The sealing agent is secondary or a sub-component of the item that is sealed.

In either of the above cases, once the item is sealed or sealed up, the item and the seal remain inextricably connected! However, the item being sealed is more important and sealing it up ensures that it is made secure and understood to be credible and authentic. Since the seventy weeks explicitly seals up the *châzôwn and the prophecy,* the seventy weeks becomes the secondary or sub-component of that which is to be sealed, i.e., the *châzôwn* of Chapter 8; but cannot be removed or separated from it. They are inseparable! But, what about *the prophecy*? Gabriel plainly states that there are two items that are to be sealed by the seventy weeks, they are the *châzôwn and the prophecy*. The *châzôwn* has already been determined to be the narrative of Daniel Chapter 8:1-14; but what is the prophecy to which it is linked? The answer can be found in Gabriel's own words as he speaks of the life, ministry and death of Messiah. Gabriel plainly prophesies of the long-awaited Messiah. The arrival of Messiah according to these prophetic words of Gabriel would validate this seventy weeks prophecy and it would in turn, authenticate and make sure the *châzôwn* of Daniel Chapter 8.

Now that Gabriel has linked the seventy weeks prophecy[47] to the *châzôwn*. He then speaks of the one start point of both:

> *Dan9:25 Know therefore and understand, that from the going forth of the commandment to restore and to build Jerusalem unto the Messiah the Prince shall be seven weeks, and threescore and two weeks: . . .*

There are but four historical events which can be taken as potentially answering the commandment to restore and build Jerusalem and then using this start point of each to find Messiah.[48] These historical events and start points are:

(1)   The decree of Cyrus for the rebuilding of the house of God, B.C. 536 (Ezra 1:1-4; 5:13).

(2)   The decree of Darius for the continuing of that work, which had been hindered, B.C. 520 (Ezra 6:1-12).

(3)   The decree of Artaxerxes to Ezra in his seventh year, B.C. 457 (Ezra 7:11-28).

---

[47] Note: For a detailed study of this seventy weeks prophecy, see the systematic study entitled, *Roots of Evangelical Lies!*

[48] Note: There are several well documented scholarly views on the identity of Messiah from this Daniel passage. This study follows the biblical prescription by allowing the Bible to speak for itself and to evidence Messiah, i.e., the Anointed One after the *seven-weeks, and threescore and two weeks* of prophetic time.

(4) The grant to Nehemiah from Artaxerxes in his twentieth year, B.C. 444. (Nehemiah 2).[49]

Aside from those who affix the seventy weeks to the Maccabean period, the approach to finding Messiah consistent with this seventy weeks prophetic period is to use each of the above dates as the start point of this seventy weeks prophecy and at the terminus of 69 of these weeks to determine מָשִׁיחַ, Messiah.[50] This period, *seven weeks, and threescore and two weeks* is accounted as 69 weeks. This period, 69 weeks multiplied by 7 days, equals 483 days, which is understood as 483 years.[51]   Using 483 years as a constant, the following calculations is set forth in order to determine Messiah at its terminus:

---

[49] Note: This is termed a grant as Artaxerxes had granted Nehemiah according to his request. This was not a royal decree as that which was given by

Cyrus, Darius and Artaxerxes. In the narrative between Nehemiah and Artaxerxes "decree" is not rendered.

[50] מָשִׁיחַ, mâshîyach, maw-shee'-akh; from H4886; anointed; usually a consecrated person (as a king, priest, or saint); specifically, the Messiah:— anointed, Messiah. Strong's Concordance with Hebrew and Greek Lexicon, accessed July, 15, 2020, https://www. blueletterbible.org/ lang/Lexicon/ Lexicon.cfm?strongs=H4899&t=KJV. Note: The Hebrew word Messiah is only used in the book of Daniel. Correspondingly, the Greek for Messiah, Anointed One, is used in the New Testament regarding Christ who was anointed by the Holy Spirit, Acts 10:38, Luke 4:18 & Heb. 1:9.

[51] Note: Different schools of thought use different methods to arrive at this same conclusion, i.e., the seventy weeks prophecy must be accounted as years in order to reach the periphery of Messiah (Anointed One).

Cyrus [The Great]	Darius [The Great]	Artaxerxes [Longimanus]	Artaxerxes [Longimanus]
536bc	520bc	457bc	444bc
+483	+483	+483	+483
53bc	37bc	26ad	39ad

With the above calculations, it can be observed that the decrees of Cyrus and Darius fall short of the periphery of Messiah / the Anointed One by many years (i.e., the end point comes prior to Messiah / Christ) and are therefore discounted as being relevant to the terminus of these 483 prophetic years. With the other two calculations, it must be noted that when calculating across the BC/AD timeline there is a need to adjust each by 1 as there is no year zero. Consequently, the decree by Artaxerxes, given in 457bc, after 483 years would find its terminus in 27ad and the grant, given to Nehemiah by the same Artaxerxes in 444, would terminate in 39ad.

Another caveat to these calculations is worth mentioning. Those who use Artaxerxes' 444bc date as the start point of the seventy weeks prophecy use a variant method of calculation developed by Robert Anderson and controversially arrive, after 483 years, at 32ad instead of 39ad. This end point they mark as the triumphant entry of Jesus into Jerusalem.[52] However, whether reckoning the 32ad or the 39ad as finding Messiah, both dates fail to fulfill the prophecy for this simple reason. The only date given in the Scripture regarding Jesus (Messiah), while on earth is Luke

---

[52] Robert Anderson, *The Coming Prince*, (Lawton, CA: Trumpet Press, 2012).

3:1, *the 15th year of Tiberius Caesar.*[53] In this year Jesus was baptized.[54] This date has been recorded historically as either 26ad or 27ad. By piecing together Jesus' attendance at Passover, it has been determined that He attended the most three or four. Using these parameters liberally, 27ad plus 4 years would take us to 31ad. Since Jesus left the earth some forty days after the Passover in the year He was crucified, liberally accounted as 31ad, both dates of 32ad and 39ad would fail as Jesus would have already left the earth. [55]

Additionally, those who subscribe to Anderson's method of calculation also suggest that the seventy weeks prophecy contains a gap and has therefore not yet and will not find terminus until the Second Coming of Jesus. Following this line of reasoning, it would yet be another challenge to determine how the seventy weeks prophecy, which cannot be extricated from the two thousand three hundred days prophecy, would then seal up the *châzôwn*?

Returning to Gabriel's statements:

---

[53] Note: During the Second Temple era, the Jews adopted the Syro Macedonian calendaring system, this placed the end of Tiberius' 1st renal year in 14ad and the end of his 15th year at the end of 28ad. This calendar year began in the autumn of each year. This would place the beginning of his 15th renal year in the autumn of 27ad.

[54] Note: Luke records that at Jesus' baptism, He was anointed with the Holy Ghost. Luke 4:18.

[55] Note: Futurism and its corollary Dispensationalism both subscribe to this view; however, as can be reckoned by a correct understanding of the châzôwn both 32ad and 39ad are incorrect terminuses of the 483 years when seeking to find Messiah.

Dan9:24 Seventy weeks are châthak upon thy people and upon thy holy city . . . and to châtham the châzôwn and prophecy.

Dan9:25 Know therefore and understand, that from the going forth of the commandment to restore and to build Jerusalem unto the Messiah the Prince shall be seven weeks, and threescore and two weeks: . . .

The only decree that fits the prophetic timeline would be that of Artaxerxes in 457bc. There would be seventy weeks cut off, beginning from the going forth of the command to restore and to build Jerusalem. This command would be issued by Artaxerxes in 457bc and sixty-nine weeks of years afterward, Messiah, the Anointed One would be presented to the world, anointed by the Holy Spirit at His baptism. This 483-year period would end in 27ad. This would constitute 69 of the 70 weeks. After these seven, plus sixty-two weeks Messiah would then be כָּרַת *kârath*[56] in the midst of the (final) week. According to the seventy weeks prophecy, Jesus' ministry would extend from 27ad to 31ad, a total of three and a half years. Now, three and a half years after the cutting off of Messiah these prophetic days of the seventy-weeks would end. Having been thus established by its three periodic

---

[56] כָּרַת kârath, kaw-rath'; a primitive root; to cut (off, down or asunder); by implication, to destroy or consume; specifically, to covenant (i.e. make an alliance or bargain, originally by cutting flesh and passing between the pieces):—be chewed, be con-(feder-) ate, covenant, cut (down, off), destroy, fail, feller, be freed, hew (down), make a league (covenant), lose, perish, utterly, want. Strong's Concordance with Hebrew and Greek Lexicon, accessed July, 15, 2020, https://www. blueletterbible.org/ lang/Lexicon/ Lexicon.cfm?strongs=H3772&t=KJV.

indicators,[57] this seventy weeks prophecy would find its terminus in 34ad.

However, being that which seals up the *châzôwn,* these seventy weeks are then a sub-component of the *châzôwn.* There had remained only two components of the *châzôwn* that Gabriel had not interpreted to Daniel. These were (1) regarding the two thousand three hundred days and (2) the cleansing of the sanctuary. These were also the same subjects, time and the sanctuary, for which Daniel had sought to understand by studying Jeremiah's seventy-year prophecy and its relationship to the rebuilding of the sanctuary at Jerusalem. Once the seal, which is the seventy weeks, authenticates the prophecy regarding the earthly life, ministry and death of Messiah, then that which it seals up, *the châzôwn of the evening and the morning,* is determined to be secured / made sure.

The sanctuary that is to be cleansed must therefore be located at the end of the two thousand three hundred days as the seventy weeks are cut from these two thousand three hundred days.[58] Here an undeniable fact must be reckoned with, since the seventy weeks prophecy seals up the *châzôwn* and these seventy weeks find terminus in the periphery of Messiah, then the two thousand three hundred days from which these seventy weeks are cut off cannot be reckoned as literal days ending with Antiochus IV Epiphanes in the Maccabean period. To be consistent with the

---

[57] Note: This 70weeks prophecy is made up of three segments: seven weeks and threescore and two weeks and one week (Dan9:24-27).

[58] Note: Preterism, subscribes to the view that both the two thousand three hundred days and the seventy weeks prophecies terminate during the Maccabean period and is tied in some way to Antiochus IV Epiphanes; however, no Preterist calculations have yet been forwarded to account for the exactness of the 7+62+1 weeks. Some have even forwarded that the author of Daniel miscalculated (i.e., a chronological miscalculation on [the] part of the writer).

time element of the seal, i.e., the seventy weeks prophecy, the two thousand three hundred days must be reckoned as years. In other words, since the seventy weeks are a sub-component of the two thousand three hundred days, and its terminus is in the periphery of Messiah, then the end point of the two thousand three hundred days, at which the sanctuary will be cleansed must also find terminus beyond the periphery of Messiah! This will be further unpacked later in the study.

9: Understanding the *Dâbar*

In order to forensically understand Daniel's vision of the *châzôwn*, it is most important to see the big picture. The *châzôwn* was given in the 3rd year of King Belshazzar of Babylon. It contained some visual elements and an auditory element of which the visual elements were explained by Gabriel at the time that the *châzôwn* was given to Daniel. The auditory element, the conversation between the two angels, i.e., the *dâbar*, was not explained at that time because the prophet had fainted. There are several variant comments regarding the mentioning of the palace of Shushan and the River Ulai in conjunction with this *châzôwn*. Nevertheless, Daniel says:

> *Dan8:2 And I saw in a châzôwn; and it came to pass, when I saw, that I was at Shushan in the palace, which is in the province of Elam; and I saw in a châzôwn, and I was by the river of Ulai.*

Arguably, the language of the text does not definitely endorse either position as to whether Daniel was at the location described or at some other unknown location; however, when Daniel's documentation of his other visionary experiences are taken into consideration, it becomes increasingly obvious that Daniel on every occasion detailed not only the "vision" that was given to him but also the location where the "vision" was given:

> *Dan2:17 Then Daniel went to his house, and made the thing known to Hananiah, Mishael, and Azariah, his companions: ^{18} that they would desire mercies of the God of heaven concerning this secret; that Daniel and his fellows*

should not perish with the rest of the wise men of Babylon. ¹⁹ Then was the secret revealed unto Daniel in a night vision. Then Daniel blessed the God of heaven.

In this first vision, when he was given the *chêzêv* of the Great Metal Man, Daniel was at this house and in his bed, asleep.

> *Dan7:1 In the first year of Belshazzar king of Babylon Daniel had a dream and visions of his head upon his bed: then he wrote the dream, and told the sum of the matters.*

In his second vision, when he was given the *chêzêv* of the Four Great Beasts from the Sea. Daniel was asleep. More than likely Daniel was again at this house and in his bed, asleep.

In his fourth and final vision, Daniel states:

> *Dan10:4 And in the four and twentieth day of the first month, as I was by the side of the great river, which is Hiddekel . . .*

In each of the above references, Daniel details his location. If it is not accepted that Daniel was at the location detailed in the *châzôwn,* this would then be an inconsistency in Daniel's writings. Additionally there would be no way to determine just where the prophet was when he received the *châzôwn.* The importance of recognizing Daniel's location is evident when the bigger picture of the *châzôwn* is taken into consideration.

This study forwards that the prophet Daniel had a *châzôwn* that is detailed in Daniel 8:1-14. It is the only visionary experience occasioned by the prophet for which he uses the word *châzôwn* and that the exposé regarding the same spans the rest of the book of Daniel. When searching for an understanding of the elements of this *châzôwn, Daniel says:*

> *Dan8:15* *. . . behold, there stood before me as the appearance of a man. And I heard a man's voice between the banks of Ulai, which called, and said, Gabriel, make this man to understand the vision.*

There are now four divine beings present at this, the beginning of Gabriel's explanation of the *châzôwn*. Two are mentioned in the passage above, the other two in the passage below:

> *Dan8:13* *Then I heard one saint speaking, and another saint said unto that certain saint which spake, How long shall be the châzôwn concerning the daily sacrifice, and the transgression of desolation, to give both the sanctuary and the host to be trodden under foot?*

There is also a body of water. In this the beginning of Gabriel's explanation, it is the River Ulai. These descriptions mark the beginning of Gabriel's exposition of the *châzôwn* as directed by the man's voice from the river to make Daniel understand.

As was mentioned at the outset of this study, the original language had no syntactical punctuations so other means had to be employed so as to determine where things started and where they ended. The question that should now be asked is this. Is there a corresponding scene that would demark the ending of Gabriel's exposition of the *châzôwn?* And the answer is, yes. In Daniel 12:5, when Gabriel had finished his unbroken interpretive speech narrative, (11:1-12:4), Daniel writes:

> *Dan12:5* *Then I Daniel looked, and, behold, there stood other two, the one on this side of the bank of the river, and the other on that side of the bank of the river.* *6 And one said to the man clothed in linen, which was upon the waters of the river, How long shall it be to the end of these wonders* *7 And I heard the man clothed in linen,*

which was upon the waters of the river, when he held up his right hand and his left hand unto heaven, and sware by him that liveth for ever that it shall be for a time, times, and an half; and when he shall have accomplished to scatter the power of the holy people, all these things shall be finished.

Here again there are four divine beings. Two upon either side of the River Hiddekel (ch10:4), Gabriel, and the man that is upon the water. It is the identical scene that was depicted at the outset of Gabriel's exposé of the *châzôwn*. In both instances there are four divine beings, a body of water and intermingled conversation between them. The takeaway here is this, if Daniel was at an unknown location, there would be no literary justification to bookend the *châzôwn* with these two identical scenes. Additionally, if the entire scene at the outset of the *châzôwn* was not literally located at the River Ulai, again there would be no justification to end Gabriel's exposé with the very sane scene with which it had begun. These two identical physical scenes, these bookends begin and end Gabriel's exposé of the *châzôwn* that was given to Daniel in ch8:1-14.

Upon his return to Daniel in Chapter 9, Gabriel continues to speak of this *dâbâr* when he said:

> **Dan9:23** . . . *therefore understand the dâbâr, and consider the mar'eh.*

It was after making the above statement that Gabriel had spoken to Daniel about time (seventy weeks) and the sanctuary (anoint the most Holy), the very elements of the *châzôwn* that had not been explained to Daniel before. In effect, Gabriel began to bring Daniel an understanding regarding the conversation which had been a part of the *châzôwn*. However, it was not until Chapter 10 that Daniel says he finally got it!

Dan10:1 . . . *he understood the dâbâr, and had understanding of the mar'eh*

Although the word *châzôwn* is not expressly mentioned in Chapter 12, by dismissing the embedded chapter break and following the unbroken interpretive speech narrative, it is the *châzôwn* of which Gabriel continues to speak regarding. There is, however, an obvious break at ch12:3 as Gabriel ends his unbroken interpretative speech narrative and now gives Daniel a directive:

Dan12:4 *But thou, O Daniel, shut up the words, and seal the book, even to the time of the end: many shall run to and fro, and knowledge shall be increased.*

Here at the end of his unbroken interpretive speech narrative, Gabriel tells Daniel to *shut up the words*. Gabriel had already told Daniel at the beginning of his exposition of the *châzôwn* that he was to *shut up the châzôwn for it shall be for many days* (Dan8:26). Additionally, he was told to *seal the book, even to the time of the end* (Dan 12:4). Gabriel now tells Daniel more specifically:

Dan12:9 . . . *Go thy way, Daniel: for the dâbâr are closed up and sealed till the time of the end.*

Without a doubt, there is something regarding Daniel's writings that is to remain for *many days* even to *the time of the end*. The original word Gabriel uses here for "words" is *dâbâr*. It is the same that he had used before, when speaking to Daniel regarding the auditory portion of the *châzôwn:*

Dan8:13 *Then I heard one saint dâbâr, and another saint said unto that certain saint which dâbâr. . .*

Dan9:23 . . . *therefore understand the dâbâr, and consider the mar'eh.*

Dan10:1 . . . *he understood the dâbâr, and had understanding of the mar'eh*

Dan12:4 *But thou, O Daniel, shut up the dâbâr, and seal the book, even to the time of the end:*

Dan12:9 *And he said, Go thy way, Daniel: for the dâbâr are closed up and châtham till the time of the end.*

Reflecting on the comments in this study regarding Dan8:27, it was the *dâbar* of ch8:13, 14, which Daniel had not understood. The visual components of the *châzôwn* had been interpreted by Gabriel; however, the audio-visual component, i.e., the observed conversation between the two saints, was not then interpreted to Daniel. The most probable reason why an explanation had not been given to Daniel was because Daniel had fainted. Subsequently, Daniel had sought for an understanding of this time element spoken of in the *châzôwn* by studying Jeremiah's writings to *understand by books the number of years, whereby the Lord would accomplish seventy years in the desolation of Jerusalem* (Dan9:2). In his subsequent conversation with Daniel in ch9:24, Gabriel begins the explanation of the *dâbar* in the *châzôwn*. It is this *dâbar,* which Daniel referenced at the beginning of Gabriel's unbroken speech monologue (ch10:1) and which Gabriel now references here at its end. Here at the end of his exposé, he tells Daniel to shut up the *dâbar* and that the *dâbar* are closed up *till the time of the end, (Dan12:4, 9).*

The takeaway here is that, although the interpretation of the *dâbar* in the *châzôwn* regarding the 2300 days and the sanctuary that had to be cleansed, had been given to and recorded by Daniel, the understanding of same by his readers would remain until *the time of the end.* Consequently, the sanctuary that was to be cleansed would also not find understanding nor fulfillment until *the time of the end* had come. Additionally, Daniel was told to *châtham (to seal up) the book, even to the time of the end* (Dan12:4). A careful review of the language used by the writer and the "visions" recorded would underscore that the *châzôwn* is the book in mention as it covers Daniel 8-12 and is written completely in Hebrew. In essence, the book of Daniel's *châzôwn,* particularly the *dâbâr* regarding the time elements and the sanctuary would not be understood nor occur until *the time of the end* had come.

10: Daniel's Great *Mar'âh*

Daniel's next visionary encounter comes in the 10th Chapter of Daniel. It is now the 3rd year of Cyrus the Great. In this chapter, the writer uses three different words for "vision", *mar'eh, mar'âh and châzôwn*. These words are used in the following context:

> *Dan10:1 In the third year of Cyrus king of Persia a thing was revealed unto Daniel, whose name was called Belteshazzar; and the thing was true, but the time appointed was long: and he understood the thing, and had understanding of the mar'eh.*

> *Dan10:7 And I Daniel alone saw the mar'âh: for the men that were with me saw not the mar'âh; but a great quaking fell upon them, so that they fled to hide themselves.*

> *Dan10:8 Therefore I was left alone, and saw this great mar'âh, and there remained no strength in me: for my comeliness was turned in me into corruption, and I retained no strength.*

> *Dan10:14 Now I am come to make thee understand what shall befall thy people in the latter days: for yet the châzôwn is for many days.*

> *Dan10:16 And, behold, one like the similitude of the sons of men touched my lips: then I opened my mouth, and spake, and said unto him that stood before me, O my lord, by the mar'âh my sorrows are turned upon me, and I have retained no strength.*

There can be no denying that Daniel had a visionary experience here in Chapter 10, in the 3rd year of Cyrus, as he clearly says he saw the *mar'âh (vision: mode of revelation)*. Further, the men that were with him saw not the *mar'âh*, therefore he was left alone and saw this great *mar'âh*.

Something extraordinary and different occurs here by the River Hiddekel. So extraordinary that the men that were with Daniel, because of fear, fled to hide themselves and Daniel fell upon the ground as though he were dumb and without strength. Daniel records just what he saw in this great *mar'âh*:

> *Dan10:5 then I lifted up mine eyes, and looked, and behold a certain man clothed in linen, whose loins were girded with fine gold of Uphaz: 6 his body also was like the beryl, and his face as the appearance of lightning, and his eyes as lamps of fire, and his arms and his feet like in colour to polished brass, and the voice of his words like the voice of a multitude.*

In recording this experience, Daniel uses a new word for "vision" to describe this unique and different experience. Here Daniel was not asleep and therefore did not have a *chêzêv* nor was he in an ecstatic state and had a *châzôwn*. Here Daniel uses *mar'âh* to describe his experience. Here again Daniel was wide awake and in the company of others who fled because a great fear (quaking) came upon them.

It is impractical to evaluate what Daniel saw at the River Hiddekel without comparing this to what John later saw, while on the isle of Patmos:

> *Rev1:13 And in the midst of the seven candlesticks one like unto the Son of man, clothed with a garment down to the foot, and girt about the paps with a golden girdle. 14 His*

*head and his hairs were white like wool, as white as snow;
and his eyes were as a flame of fire; ¹⁵ and his feet like unto
fine brass, as if they burned in a furnace; and his voice as
the sound of many waters. ¹⁶ And he had in his right hand
seven stars: and out of his mouth went a sharp two-edged
sword: and his countenance was as the sun shineth in his
strength.*

<u>**Daniel**</u>	<u>**John**</u>
Saw: *one* like the similitude of the sons of men	Saw: *one* like unto the Son of man
Clothed: Linen	Clothed: Garment
Loins: Gold of Uphaz	Loins: Golden girdle
Body: Beryl[59]	Head, hair: White as wool / white as snow
Face: Lightening	Face / countenance: sun in his strength
Eyes: Lamps of fire	Eyes: Flames of fire
Arms, feet: Polished brass	Feet: Burnt brass
Voice: like of a multitude	Voice: Sound of many waters / trumpet

Although Daniel and John did not describe the very exact features
of the individual that had appeared to each of them, those
overlapping features are remarkably similar. Additionally, the

---

[59] Note: Pure beryl is colorless.

impact upon their person, of their individual experience is definitely the same.

> Dan10:8 ... and there remained no strength in me: for my comeliness was turned in me into corruption, and I retained no strength. 9 Yet heard I the voice of his words: and ... then was I in a deep sleep on my face, and my face toward the ground. 10 And, behold, an hand touched me, which set me upon my knees and upon the palms of my hands.... 12 Then said he unto me, Fear not.

> Rev1:17 And when I saw him, I fell at his feet as dead. And he laid his right hand upon me, saying unto me, Fear not ..

Both Daniel and John came into the very presence of deity. They were both made weak and speechless but were assured by the divine One that they should fear not because they were deemed worthy, like Moses, to be in such close proximity to a divine being. Although Daniel did not fully identify this being, John says definitely that He is the One that was slain; but now lives. He is the Alpha and Omega. He is the Word of God. He is the Christ. The great *mar'âh* which Daniel saw by the River Hiddekel was that of Christ, whom Gabriel identified as Michael.

While in this great *mar'âh*, Gabriel also gives Daniel the reason for having come to him and the reason why Michael (Christ) is also come:

> Dan10:12 Then said he unto me, Fear not, Daniel: for from the first day that thou didst set thine heart to understand, and to chasten thyself before thy God, thy words were heard, and I am come for thy words. 13 But the prince of the kingdom of Persia withstood me one and twenty days: but, lo, Michael, one of the chief princes, came to help me; and I remained there with the kings of Persia. 14 Now I am

come to make thee understand what shall befall thy people in the latter days: for yet the châzôwn is for many days.

In this the 3rd year of Cyrus, Daniel had been fasting and praying, seeking for an understanding regarding *what shall befall his people in the latter days*. Daniel's prayer had been heard and Gabriel was dispatched to bring Daniel this understanding from the first day that Daniel had set his heart to understand; but Gabriel had been withstood by the prince of the kingdom of Persia until Michael had come to assist. After that encounter, Gabriel has finally reached Daniel with the understanding that he has been searching for.[60]

Note that Daniel's only use of *mar'eh* in ch10:1 of this narrative, is consistent with his previous use of this word. It refers to something other than itself. It is the thing that is seen.[61]

Dan8:16 Gabriel, make this *man* to understand the *mar'eh*.

Dan8:26 And the *mar'eh* of the evening and the morning which was told *is* true:

Dan8:27 I was astonished at the *mar'eh*, but none understood *it*.

Dan9:23 . . . understand the matter, and consider the *mar'eh*.

Dan10:1 . . . he understood the thing, and had understanding of the *mar'eh*.

---

[60] Note: For a full exposition of this issue and the reason why Daniel was fasting and praying in this the 3rd year of Cyrus, see the systematic study on *The Visions of Daniel*.

[61] Note: Mar'eh is also used in relation to countenance and appearance and not in regard to an actual visionary encounter.

Note also the similarity of the above words of Gabriel in Dan. 9:23 and that of Daniel's in 10:1 are remarkably the same. The very same phrase Gabriel had used in Chapter 9:23, Daniel now uses here in Chapter 10:1:

> *Dan10:1 In the third year of Cyrus king of Persia a dâbâr was revealed unto Daniel, whose name was called Belteshazzar; and the dâbâr was true, but the time appointed was long: and he understood the dâbâr, and had understanding of the mar'eh.*

The words *matter* from ch9:23, and *thing* from ch10:1 have been translated from the very same Hebrew word, *dâbâr*. Gabriel had said to Daniel, *understand the dâbâr, and consider the mar'eh. (ch9:23) i.e.,* 'understand the conversation, and consider that which you had seen'. In the presence of Gabriel some time later, Daniel now says, *'he understood the dâbâr, and had understanding of the mar'eh, (ch10:1) i.e.,* 'he now understood the conversation and had understanding of that which he had seen'. Daniel is letting his readers know that he now has gained an understanding of the *dâbâr*, the conversation, which he had observed in the *châzôwn:*

> *Dan8:13 Then I heard one saint dâbar, and another saint said unto that certain saint which dâbar, How long shall be the vision concerning the daily sacrifice, and the transgression of desolation, to give both the sanctuary and the host to be trodden under foot? 14 And he said unto me, Unto two thousand and three hundred days; then shall the sanctuary be cleansed.*

In this conversation between these two saints several questions were asked for which no answer has yet been provided to Daniel's readers: however, before Gabriel's upcoming monologue, 11:1-

12:4, Daniel precedes the documenting of this monologue by informing his readers that the answers are forthcoming.

The subsequent monologue given by Gabriel must then be underpinned by the said conversation between the two saints in the *châzôwn*. Any interpretation of the rest of Daniel that does not explicitly include the conversation portion of the *châzôwn* becomes untenable as a valid interpretation. While Daniel is yet in this great *mar'âh*, Gabriel speaks to him of the *châzôwn*. Gabriel's usage of *châzôwn* in ch10:14 of this passage, is consistent with the previous use of this word. It refers to the specific experience Daniel had in the 3rd year of Belshazzar, recorded in Daniel 8:1-14, at the River Ulai, while in an ecstatic state:

> *Dan8:1* . . . *a châzôwn appeared unto me, even unto me Daniel* . . .

> *Dan8:2* *And I saw in a châzôwn; . . . And I saw in a châzôwn . . .*

> *Dan8:13* . . . *How long shall be the châzôwn* . . .

> *Dan8:15* . . . *I Daniel, had seen the châzôwn* . . .

> *Dan8:17* . . . *at the time of the end shall be the châzôwn.*

> *Dan8:26* . . . *shut thou up the châzôwn; for it shall be for many days.*

> *Dan9:21* . . . *the man Gabriel, whom I had seen in the châzôwn* . . .

> *Dan9:24* *Seventy weeks are determined upon thy people and upon thy holy city . . . to seal up the châzôwn and prophecy . . .*

> *Dan10:14* . . . *for yet the châzôwn is for many days.*

Dan11:14 . . . *the robbers of thy people shall exalt themselves to establish the châzôwn; . . .*

While there are still several aspects of the *châzôwn* yet to be unpacked, what has been given by Gabriel thus far, here in Chapter 10 is that the *châzôwn* is *for many days.* However, note carefully Gabriel's words in the 3rd year of Belshazzar, that *"at the time of the end shall be the châzôwn"* (ch8:17), and "it (the *châzôwn*) shall be for many days" (ch8:26). And here in the 3rd year of Cyrus that *the time appointed was long, (ch10:1),* the *châzôwn* is yet for *many days* (ch10:14) and the *châzôwn)* has something to do *with the time of the end (ch11:35, 40; 12:4, 9).* In both of these narratives, the *châzôwn* has been similarly described assuring the reader of the direct correlation between Gabriel's interpretations of the actual *châzôwn* in Daniel 8:15-26 and Gabriel's return in Daniel 10:1 - 12:13.

In Chapter 8 of this study, it was shown that the seventy weeks prophecy was given to seal up / make sure / verify the *châzôwn and prophecy.* The seventy weeks were determined / cut off from the *châzôwn,* which began with the going forth of the command to restore and build Jerusalem. This command was given by Artaxerxes in 457bc and its *terminus ad quem* (ending date) would have been in 34ad. These seventy weeks being that which seals up / makes sure / verifies the *châzôwn* would mean that the *châzôwn* is yet for many days beyond that which has sealed it. In referencing the *châzôwn,* here in the great *mar'âh* of Chapter 10, Gabriel expressly links what he is about to describe to Daniel (in Chapter 11) as being connected to the *châzôwn* of Chapter 8.

11: Establishing the *Châzôwn*

After the introductory conversation with Gabriel and with the *one like the similitude of the sons of men*, which takes up the entire Chapter 10, Gabriel then says to Daniel:

> *Dan10:21* *But I will shew thee that which is noted in the scripture of truth: and there is none that holdeth with me in these things, but Michael your prince. . .*

At this junction, it is very important to note that the forthcoming monologue which Gabriel presents is consistent with the details of the *châzôwn* recorded in Daniel Chapter 8. The *châzôwn* is about a ram, an he-goat, a little horn, and a conversation regarding time and the sanctuary. It spoke about how the ram and he-goat fought and the subsequent results.

Dismissing the added chapter break, between Chapters 10 and 11 Gabriel now says:

> *Dan11:2* *And now will I shew thee the truth. Behold, there shall stand up yet three kings in Persia; and the fourth shall be far richer than they all: and by his strength through his riches he shall stir up all against the realm of Grecia. ³ And a mighty king shall stand up, that shall rule with great dominion, and do according to his will. ⁴ And when he shall stand up, his kingdom shall be broken, and shall be divided toward the four winds of heaven; and not to his posterity, nor according to his dominion which he ruled: for his kingdom shall be plucked up, even for others beside those.*

This previous as well as this foregoing passage has unmistakably been identified as events in the Media-Persian and Grecian empires, with Alexander, the Great, being the figure spoken of as the mighty king / great horn that is broken and his kingdom divided towards the four winds of heaven and not to his posterity nor will it remain intact as it will be broken up and given to others. These events in Dan. 11:2, 3 provide a direct correlation to the *châzôwn* of Chapter 8:

> *Dan8:3* *Then I lifted up mine eyes, and saw, and, behold, there stood before the river a ram which had two horns: and the two horns were high; but one was higher than the other, and the higher came up last. ⁴ I saw the ram pushing westward, and northward, and southward; so that no beasts might stand before him, neither was there any that could deliver out of his hand; but he did according to his will, and became great. ⁵ And as I was considering, behold, an he goat came from the west on the face of the whole earth, and touched not the ground: and the goat had a notable horn between his eyes. ⁶ And he came to the ram that had two horns, which I had seen standing before the river, and ran unto him in the fury of his power. ⁷ And I saw him come close unto the ram, and he was moved with choler against him, and smote the ram, and brake his two horns: and there was no power in the ram to stand before him, but he cast him down to the ground, and stamped upon him: and there was none that could deliver the ram out of his hand. ⁸ Therefore the he goat waxed very great: and when he was strong, the great horn was broken; and for it came up four notable ones toward the four winds of heaven.*

The understanding brought by Gabriel, here in Daniel 11 can be seen to be coincident with the *châzôwn* of Chapter 8. The ram is Media-Persia, (8:20) and the he-goat is Grecia, (8:21). As such, unmistakably, the kingdom of Grecia succeeds the kingdom of Media-Persia. Alexander's Grecian kingdom is divided towards the four winds of heaven. Daniel had also been made aware that before the Media-Persian Empire, the Babylonian Empire had held sway over *all dominion to the end of the earth*. Following the trajectory of the "visions" of Daniel 2, 7 and 8, there would now be one empire that is yet to come, it would be a divided empire, and markedly diverse from the others. This coming fourth kingdom would continue, in some way until the coming kingdom of God is established.

Most scholars accept that Daniel 10, 11 and 12 form one block of the narrative of the book.[62] Most of these scholars ascribe the historical events of this block of the narrative to the Maccabean period with its never-ending wars between the Seleucids and the Ptolemies, i.e., the King of the North and the King of the South, respectively. As such, some purport that the historical events of this block of the narrative ends in the Maccabean period. The King of the North is the Syrian kingdom with the person of Antiochus IV Epiphanes being the principal figure. His rage against the Jews is well documented. Other scholars present an eschatological antichrist typology in the personage of Antiochus IV Epiphanes. While it is evident that this block of the narrative begins with the Media-Persian Empire and continues for *"many days"* until *"the time of the end"* when *"Michael stand up"*, it

---

[62] "Daniel 10 – 12 is a whole unit". Alvin A. Low, *Dreams and Visions: Decrypting the Book of Daniel* (Morrisville, NC: Lulu Press, 2018), 145.

hardly seems plausible that the Maccabean period establishes the *châzôwn* for the following reasons:

Understandably, "many days" and "the time of the end" can arguably refer to any period of time; however, when studying systematically, there are some parameters that must be acknowledged and maintained without deviation:

1. There is a definable format to the narratives of Daniel's visions that should be consistently enforced as we look to understand the meaning of these symbols. This format, whether *chêzêv, mar'âh* or *châzôwn,* present a divine component at the end of each visionary experience. This divine component works like a period at the end of a paragraph or a chapter, following which, another major section would then begin. As mentioned before, the original writings contained no syntactical punctuation and therefore had to have other measures to determine where things started and where they ended. Daniel's first *chêzêv* ends with a stone cut out of the mountain without hands, which became the kingdom of God. The second *chêzêv* ends with a judgment scene and *one like the Son of man came with the clouds of heaven, and came to the Ancient of days, the judgment was set and the books were opened.* At the end of this judgment scene, the kingdom of the world is given to the saints of the most High, who reigns forever.

The *châzôwn* in the 3rd year of Belshazzar ends with the cleansing of the sanctuary. This cultic practice of the Jews[63] acknowledged the removal of sins from the sanctuary, placing

---

[63] Note: In the history of the Jews, the only occasion whereby the presence of a ram and he-goat were found together in any of their festivals is on the annual Day of Atonement, i.e., the cleansing of the sanctuary.

them upon a scapegoat which was afterward released into the wilderness. The great *mar'âh* in the 3rd year of Cyrus ends when *Michael, stands up, the great prince which standeth for the children of thy people.* The intimation is that these are parallel prophetic visionary experiences that speak to the same events but from differing perspectives.[64] Each visionary experience ends with a divine component, which evidences the Kingdom of God. Therefore, confining the narrative of Chapter 10-12 to end in the Maccabean period violates this framework that is evident in the writings of Daniel.

2. The narrative of Daniel 8-9 and 10-12 speaks of the timeline mentioned in the *châzôwn*, which stretches far beyond the Maccabean period. The two thousand three hundred days of Chapter 8 and the seventy-week prophecy in Daniel 9 are inextricably linked together by the statement of Gabriel that the seventy weeks are "cut off" from the two thousand three hundred days of the *châzôwn*. These seventy weeks also "seals up" the *châzôwn and the prophecy*. Undeniably, there is but only one *châzôwn* recorded in the entire book of Daniel and it is found in Daniel 8:1-14. These seventy weeks, generally regarded as 490 years places the *terminus ad quem* (ending date) in the periphery of Messiah, which is hundreds of years after the Maccabean period. This would intimate that the ending of the two thousand three hundred days must be accounted as years, so as to be compatible with the 490 years and are therefore even further forward in time than the periphery of Messiah. While scholars acknowledge that the seventy weeks prophecy reaches the time of Messiah, they fail

---

[64] Note: This study presents the writings of Daniel as being the work of one individual and that all the visions documented are interconnected.

to acknowledge the connection of its narrative with the actual *châzôwn* of Chapter 8. They fail to acknowledge that the seventy weeks seals up the *châzôwn and prophecy,* an inextricable link, one that cannot be broken.

Additionally, the narrative of Daniel 11, which is a continuation of Gabriel's monologue to Daniel that began in Daniel 10 makes it clear that the *châzôwn* is the "vision" that is being referenced in Daniel 11. This is what Gabriel had said to Daniel:

> *Dan10:14* *Now I am come to make thee understand what shall befall thy people in the latter days: for yet the châzôwn is for many days.*

Nowhere in Daniel 10 does Gabriel provide this understanding regarding, "what shall befall Daniel's people in the latter days"; however, in Daniel 11, Gabriel begins to provide such an understanding by unpacking the symbols that Daniel had already become familiar with from the *châzôwn* of Chapter 8. Interestingly, of all the words Daniel has used for "vision" throughout his writing, in Chapter 11 he uses only one, *châzôwn*. The takeaway here is obvious, that which shall befall Daniel's people in the latter days is wrapped up in the continuous exposé of the *châzôwn* detailed in Daniel 11. This exposition regarding Daniel's people is Gabriel's continued explanation of the *châzôwn* and of the *dâbâr* which was observed in the *châzôwn* of Daniel 8, for which the timeline is hundreds of years beyond the Maccabean period, even to the standing up of Michael and the deliverance of His people.

3. Antiochus IV Epiphanes cannot be the King of the North mentioned in Daniel for the following obvious reason.[65] The parallelism of the narrative of Daniel 11 is unquestionably the same as the *châzôwn* in Daniel 8. Both detail the rise of Grecia and the disposition of Alexander's kingdom into four parcels. Let's reason together that the King of the North in Daniel 11 is Syria and its kings and that the King of the South is Egypt and all their kings. The two other original kingdoms formed from Alexander's kingdom would be Thrace and Macedon. These four kingdoms would then be the "four notable horns" (ch8:8) that would constitute the divided territory of Alexander's kingdom. Now "out of one of them came forth a little horn", that would perform much atrocities.[66] In Gabriel's exposition of this little horn in Daniel 8:19-26, he is called a "king of fierce countenance" (ch8:23). It would then be this king's activities that is equated with the little horn in Daniel 8 and the King of the North in Daniel 11. Now, as recorded in the Bible, Gabriel sums up the activity of the ram, by saying: *he did according to his will, and became great.* Of the he-goat Gabriel states: *the he goat waxed very great* and that the little horn *waxed exceeding great.* There is a distinct progression of greatness associated with these symbolic entities which cannot be argued away. The little horn is the greatest when compared to the ram and the he-goat; however, suggesting that the little horn is Antiochus IV

---

[65] Note: For a complete survey of Antiochus IV Epiphanes in relation to Daniel's little horn, see the study entitled, *Antiochus IV Epiphanes is Dead.*

[66] Note: It is purported that the little horn arose from the Syrian horn or Syrian kingdom in the person of Antiochus IV Epiphanes. For additional details on this controversial point, please see the systematic study, *Antiochus IV Epiphanes is Dead.*

Epiphanes flies in the face of the prophecy and stand in direct contradiction to the actual words of Gabriel in this very passage:

> *Dan8:21 And the rough goat is the king of Grecia: and the great horn that is between his eyes is the first king. 22 Now that being broken, whereas four stood up for it, <u>four kingdoms shall stand up out of the nation, but not in his power.</u>*

Pause here for a minute and think about this for a moment. The four kingdoms that stood up out of the nation of Grecia were Syria, Egypt, Thrace and Macedon. Here Gabriel states unequivocally that none of these named kingdoms will rise to the greatness, nor have the power which Alexander, the Great had. That is to say none of these four kingdoms can be greater than Alexander's kingdom. Associating Antiochus IV Epiphanes with the little horn violates this expressed statement of Gabriel as Antiochus IV Epiphanes, a king of Syria, cannot be exceedingly greater than Alexander the Great and at the same time, not be as powerful as him. Additionally, of all the Seleucid kings, history evidenced that it was his grandfather who was dubbed Antiochus III the Great!

Without violating these obvious parameters, search must be made beyond the Maccabean period for an entity akin to the Babylonian, Media-Persian and Grecian empires that would fit the detailed description ascribed in the text without violating any of the above parameters. Such a kingdom would, according to the prophetic word, in some way, continue until the kingdom of God is set up. Just as the seventy weeks sealed up the *châzôwn and prophecy,* the rise and fall of such an entity would establish the validity of the *châzôwn.* Here in Chapter 11, Daniel uses only one word for "vision", *châzôwn.* The narrative of the *châzôwn* is located in Daniel Chapter 8:1-14. The key elements are a ram, he-goat, a little horn and a conversation between two heavenly beings. The understanding emanating from the narrative of Daniel 11 must therefore conform to these elements from the *châzôwn*. Thus far in Daniel Chapter 11:1-13, Gabriel has commented upon the Ram and the He-goat. Following the trajectory of the *châzôwn*, the expectation is that his next comment will be regarding the little horn/king of fierce countenance:

> *Dan11:14* And in those times there shall many stand up against the king of the south: also the robbers of thy people shall exalt themselves to establish the châzôwn; but they shall fall.

Prior to this statement, Chapter 11 speaks of the continued warfare between the Seleucids and the Ptolemies, i.e. the King of the North and the King of the South. This seemingly never-ending battle is suddenly punctuated with a new character, *the robbers of thy people*. The primary meaning of this word, פָּרִיץ, *p^erîyts*[67] is: *violent one, breaker*. While Daniel has no record of anyone that robs in his writing, he does have record of a kingdom that breaks:

> *Dan2:40* And the fourth kingdom shall be strong as iron: forasmuch as iron breaketh in pieces and subdueth all things: and as iron that breaketh all these, shall it break in pieces and bruise.

> *Dan7:23* Thus he said, The fourth beast shall be the fourth kingdom upon earth, which shall be diverse from all

---

[67] פָּרִיץ, p^erîyts, per-eets'; from H6555; violent, i.e. a tyrant:—destroyer, ravenous, robber. Strong's Concordance with Hebrew and Greek Lexicon, accessed Sept, 23, 2020, https://www. blueletterbible.org/ lang/Lexicon/ Lexicon.cfm?strongs=H6530&t=KJV.

kingdoms, and shall devour the whole earth, and shall
tread it down, and break it in pieces.

In both the *chêzêv* of Chapter 2 and the *chêzêv* of Chapter 7, Daniel details the fourth kingdom as one that breaks. Because the *châzôwn* is a parallel prophecy, it would naturally speak of this same violent kingdom:

> *Dan8:24* *And his (the little horn/king of fierce countenance)*
> *power shall be mighty, but not by his own power: and he*
> *shall destroy wonderfully, and shall prosper, and practise,*
> *and shall destroy the mighty and the holy people.*

When all the details of the fourth kingdom of the *chêzêv* in Chapter 2 and that of the *chêzêv* in Chapter 7 along with the little horn in the *châzôwn* of Chapter 8 are examined in parallel, it will be determine that these descriptions are aligned with the same entity, *the robbers / breakers of thy people* (Dan 11:14) of which Daniel is here speaking.

Also, in this Dan11:14 statement are two vital and important concepts. This statement points to a two-dimensional concept, a horizontal plane and a vertical plane. The robbers / breakers and the self-exaltation of this kingdom. On a horizontal plain it is the robber / breaker / persecutor of God's people, and on the vertical plain it exalts itself. This kingdom is different. While the other kingdoms maintained a horizontal trajectory, this kingdom's trajectory is both horizontal and vertical. Its vertical descriptions are as follows:

> *Dan7:8* *I considered the horns, and, behold, there came up*
> *among them another little horn . . . in this horn were eyes*
> *like the eyes of man, and a mouth speaking great things.*

Dan7:11 *I beheld then because of the voice of the great words which the horn spake:*

Dan7:20 *. . . even of that horn that had eyes, and a mouth that spake very great things . . .*

Dan7:25 *And he (the little horn) shall speak great words against the most High . . .*

Dan8:11 *Yea, he (the little horn) magnified himself even to the prince of the host . . .*

Dan8:25 *And through his (the little horn) policy also he shall cause craft to prosper in his hand; and he (the little horn) shall magnify himself in his heart . . . he (the little horn) shall also stand up against the Prince of princes;*

Here in the vertical description of this entity, is a kingdom that is not aligned to God as it causes מִרְמָה, craft[68] to prosper and speak great words against God, magnify himself in his heart, even to the Prince of the host and stand up against the Prince of princes. Based on the trajectory of the visionary experiences of Daniel, he here speaks of the kingdom that rules universally after Grecia. Rome, the iron monarchy enters the prophetic narrative of Chapter 11 at verse 14 as the robbers/breakers of God's people.

Inasmuch as the seventy weeks prophecy seals up the *châzôwn and prophecy,* the alignment of the narrative of Daniel Chapter 11 with that of the *châzôwn* of Daniel Chapter 8 along

---

[68] מִרְמָה, mirmâh, meer-maw'; from H7411 in the sense of deceiving; fraud:—craft, deceit (-ful, -fully), false, feigned, guile, subtilly, treachery. Strong's Concordance with Hebrew and Greek Lexicon, accessed Nov, 17, 2020, https://www. blueletterbible.org/ lang/Lexicon/ Lexicon.cfm?strongs= H4820 &t=KJV.

with the historicity of Rome in the prophetic stream of time establishes the *châzôwn*. It was in the 3rd year of Belshazzar that Daniel was given the *châzôwn,* which he was told to seal it up until *the time of the end.* The *châzôwn* would be *for many days* and that *the time appointed was long.* These phrases connote a very long period of time. As determined by the seventy weeks prophecy, which is aligned with portions of the *châzôwn,* it speaks of events beyond the Maccabean period and reaches even unto the empire of Rome.

In the *chêzêv* of Chapter 2, the fourth kingdom is described as a divided kingdom. Not only is there a major division implied by its two legs, its feet also are composed of iron and clay and finally there are ten toes. On the head of the fourth beast in the *chêzêv* of Chapter 7, can be found ten horns. Among the ten horns of the fourth beast, there is a little horn that uproots three and takes aim at God. This little horn is also mentioned in the *châzôwn* of Chapter 8 as the king of fierce countenance. All of these parallel narratives provide a full description of the empire that comes after Grecia. This is the iron monarchy of the Roman Empire.

Although the narrative after ch11:14 plunges back into the seemingly never-ending battle of the king of the north and south, a window is opened at verses 20 and 23.

> *Dan11:20* . . . a raiser of taxes *in* the glory of the kingdom

This text complemented by Luke 3:1 speaks of the taxation of Rome in the glory days of Augustus Caesar.

> *Dan11:22* . . . and shall be broken; yea, also the prince of the covenant.

Messiah/Christ, the Prince of the covenant, as mentioned in ch9:25-27 was broken/crucified/cut off during "the midst of the week" on a Roman cross and by Roman hands. Historical references provide undeniable documentation that it was during the fourth kingdom that Messiah was evidenced and also crucified.

Further along in the narrative of Daniel 11, evidence of a shift in the trajectory of this kingdom takes place as described in these verses:

Dan11:28 . . . *and his heart shall be against the holy covenant*

Dan11:30 . . . *and have indignation against the holy covenant . . . and have intelligence with them that forsake the holy covenant.*

Dan11:32 *And such as do wickedly against the covenant shall he corrupt by flatteries:*

Throughout his writing, Daniel uses one word for covenant: בְּרִית, *bᵉrîyth.*[69] It most definitely involves the cutting of flesh as without the cutting of flesh there is no covenant. When the flesh of Christ was cut on the cross, it signified the confirmation of the promised covenant, which had been symbolized in the ancient animal sacrifices that one day Messiah would come:

Isa53:5 *But he was wounded for our transgressions, he was bruised for our iniquities: the chastisement of our peace was upon him; and with his stripes we are healed.*

This is a fundamental truth in the gospel of salvation to be taught and proclaimed to all humanity; but, here in this fourth kingdom

---

[69] בְּרִית, bᵉrîyth, ber-eeth'; from H1262 (in the sense of cutting [like H1254]); a compact (because made by passing between pieces of flesh):— confederacy, (con-) feder(-ate), covenant, league. Strong's Concordance with Hebrew and Greek Lexicon, accessed July, 15, 2020, https://www. blueletterbible.org/ lang/Lexicon/ Lexicon.cfm?strongs=H1285&t=KJV.

can elements be found of indignations against such truths. Of this fourth kingdom, in the personage of a little horn, Daniel says:

Dan8:12 *. . . and it cast down the truth to the ground; and it practised, and prospered.*

The history of Rome goes back to its alleged foundation by Romulus and Remus about the 8th century BC. It was most likely ruled by kings which was replaced by a republic and then by emperors. It was during the reign of Emperor Constantine that the first major division was evidenced as the capital of Rome was moved east to Constantinople and over time another division took place as the paganism of the empire gave way to Christianity.[70] This division of the empire into east and west saw the eventual decline of the west as barbarian tribes carved up the western / old Roman Empire and settled therein. The last Roman emperor of the west abdicated in 476ad. It was during this breakup that Rome began to be governed by the Roman bishops who with the alliance of the Eastern Roman Empire routed from its territories those that did not subscribe to the beliefs and practices that were promoted by the western Roman bishops. Persecution and annihilation were the norm for such unbelief. These bishops were subsequently called pontiffs and "pagan" (the emperors) Rome became "papal" (the priests) Rome.

Whether it is accepted that there are symbolic elements in Daniel 10, 11 and 12 that reflect Pagan and Papal Rome, the honest seeker of truth must look beyond the Maccabean period for a fulfillment of the events described in this narrative. As will be seen later in the study, the *châzôwn* is about time, i.e., God's time.

---

[70] Note: While the first division is evidenced in the geography of the kingdom, the second is evidenced in time as its customs changed from Pagan Rome to Papal Rome. From the iron monarchy to miry clay.

God's prophetic timetable and the rise and fall of Rome, although prophesied while Rome was yet a small city state, establishes the authenticity and timespan of the *châzôwn*.

12: The Time of The End

The phrase *"the time of the end"* is found nowhere else in the Scripture outside of the book of Daniel and more pointedly, nowhere else except in the *châzôwn* and subsequent expositions regarding it:

> *Dan8:17* *So he came near where I stood: and when he came, I was afraid, and fell upon my face: but he said unto me, Understand, O son of man: for at <u>the time of the end</u> shall be the châzôwn.*

> *Dan11:35* *And some of them of understanding shall fall, to try them, and to purge, and to make them white, even to <u>the time of the end</u>: because it is yet for a time appointed.*

> *Dan11:40* *And at <u>the time of the end</u> shall the king of the south push at him: and the king of the north shall come against him like a whirlwind, with chariots, and with horsemen, and with many ships; and he shall enter into the countries, and shall overflow and pass over.*

> *Dan12:4* *But thou, O Daniel, shut up the words, and seal the book, even to <u>the time of the end</u>: many shall run to and fro, and knowledge shall be increased.*

> *Dan12:9* *And he said, Go thy way, Daniel: for the words [of the châzôwn] are closed up and sealed till <u>the time of the end</u>.*

While there is much to unpack in these statements, there are some obvious takeaways that can immediately be highlighted:

1. Daniel's *châzôwn* has something to do with the *"time of the end"*.
2. Some who understand God's words will be persecuted *"even to the time of the end"* for *"the time of the end"* is yet for a time appointed.
3. At *"the time of the end"* there will be a conflict between the King of the North and the King of the South.
4. The *"time of the end"* is denoted when knowledge shall be increased.
5. Something to do with Daniel's words/writing was closed up and sealed until *"the time of the end"*.

Another way to restate these points is to say that the *châzôwn* shall be for many days[71] and reaches even to *"the time of the end"*[72], which is *yet for a time appointed*. Because the words of the book are sealed up[73] until *"the time of the end"*, it is only then that the full knowledge of Daniel's writings pertaining to God's timetable will be understood. To validate this appointed time, there will be a noted persecution of God's people up to that time by the King of the North. At the *"time of the end"*, there will also be a conflict between the kings of the North and South. When all these coordinating points intersect, God's prophetic timetable would have arrived at *"the time of the end"*.

---

71 *Dan8:26* . . . wherefore shut thou up the *châzôwn*; for it *shall be* for many days.

72 *Dan8:17* . . . *for at the time of the end shall be the châzôwn.*

73 *Dan9:24* . . . seal up the châzôwn . . . / *Dan12:4* seal the book indicates that the châzôwn is the book, written in Hebrew that was sealed / shut up until the time of the end.

A reminder that the *châzôwn* was recorded by the prophet in Daniel 8; but is explicitly mentioned subsequently in Daniel 9, 10, 11 and inferred in Daniel 12. The portion of the *châzôwn* that had to do with the conversation between the two angels was not explained to Daniel at the time when the *châzôwn* was given, so Gabriel returned in Daniel 9 to begin the explanation of this auditory component of the *châzôwn*. He speaks to Daniel regarding the elements of time and the sanctuary. These were the components of the conversation, which Daniel had observed in the *châzôwn;* but which had not been explained, because the prophet had fainted. Upon his return in Chapter 9, he tells Daniel that the seventy weeks (1) seals up the *châzôwn and the prophecy,* (2) begins in 457bc and (3) is cut off from the two thousand three hundred days prophecy of Daniel 8. Effectively, Gabriel speaks of the starting of the seventy weeks and the two thousand and three days as beginning at the same time, 457bc and running concurrently until 34ad where the seventy weeks terminate. The validity of the seventy weeks makes sure the *châzôwn* and also *the prophecy* regarding Messiah. The rise and fall of Rome establishes the *châzôwn*.

Summarily, in the *châzôwn* Rome is depicted as a little horn / a king of fierce countenance.[74] In 331bc, when Alexander the Great defeated the mighty Persian Army at the battle of Arbela, Rome was yet a small insignificant city state. Its conquest of the Italian peninsula did not occur until 264bc. But Rome grew into a mighty empire. In both the *chêzêv* of Chapter 2 and 7 and in the *châzôwn* of Chapter 8, Rome is the kingdom / empire subsequently

---

[74] Note: The reference here to Pagan Rome as a little horn reflects its smallness when compared to the mighty empires that were already in existence. At the time of the battle of Arbela, October 331 BCE, Rome was inconsequential.

ruling after Greece. Eventually it becomes a divided empire. Not only was Rome divided into east and west, geographically by Emperor Constantine; but, while the east continued until 1453, the west was broken/divided into what is now today, the nations of Europe. It was also divided in time when Pagan Rome gave way to Papal Rome. Daniel 11:14-29 evidenced the entrance and activity of Pagan Rome into the prophetic narrative as the *robbers/breakers of thy people*. Papal Rome is evidenced in the same narrative as those who are against God's *Holy covenant* and God's people, Daniel 11:30-45, inclusively.

Rome is also consistently described as being שְׁנָא,[75] diverse:

Dan7:7 After this I saw in the night visions, and behold a fourth beast, dreadful and terrible, and strong exceedingly; and it had great iron teeth: it devoured and brake in pieces and stamped the residue with the feet of it: and it was <u>diverse</u> from all the beasts that were before it; and it had ten horns.

Dan7:19 Then I would know the truth of the fourth beast, which was <u>diverse</u> from all the others, exceeding dreadful, whose teeth were of iron, and his nails of brass; which devoured, brake in pieces, and stamped the residue with his feet;

Dan7:23 Thus he said, The fourth beast shall be the fourth kingdom upon earth, which shall be <u>diverse</u> from all

---

[75] שְׁנָא, sheⁿâ', shen-aw'; (Aramaic) corresponding to H8132:—alter, change, (be) diverse. . Strong's Concordance with Hebrew and Greek Lexicon, accessed July, Dec 24, 2021, https://www. blueletterbible.org/ lang/Lexicon/ Lexicon.cfm?strongs= H8132 &t=KJV.

kingdoms, and shall devour the whole earth, and shall tread it down, and break it in pieces.

Dan7:24 And the ten horns out of this kingdom are ten kings that shall arise: and another shall rise after them; and he shall be <u>diverse</u> from the first, and he shall subdue three kings.

The original meaning of this word is to alter or change. Rome altered what was accepted / considered as normative in the ruler-ship of earthly empires. While Pagan Rome ruled on a horizontal trajectory with its pantheon of gods, Papal Rome went a step further endeavoring to rule on both a horizontal and a vertical trajectory by making itself equal with the very God of heaven.[76]

Daniel 11, although somewhat difficult to decipher, provides the detailed explanation of the *châzôwn* that was given in Daniel 8. Daniel 9 speaks of its start point coincident with the seventy weeks prophecy, which seals up the *châzôwn and prophecy,* while Daniel 11 and 12 brings the events of the *châzôwn "even to the time of the end: because it is yet for a tine appointed".* This study therefore does not altogether subscribe to that which scholars' attests, in that Daniel 10-12 is an independent unit. This study forwards that Daniel 10-12 is intricately connected to Daniel 8 and in particular, to the full exposé of the *châzôwn* and the *dâbâr* of the angels therein.

This next portion of the narrative of Daniel 11 further describes this prophesied shift of the little horn onto its vertical trajectory by speaking of how it persecutes God's people for *many*

---

[76] "We Hold Upon this earth the place of God Almighty," Pope Leo XIII, *The Great Encyclical Letters of Pope Leo XIII* (New York, NY: Benziger Brothers, 1902), 304.

days. A reminder that since Daniel 11 is underpinned by the narrative of the *châzôwn* in Daniel 8, the symbols therein will find resonance in Daniel 11. This depiction is the only one, in Daniel's narrative of Chapter 11 that speaks directly to the intense persecution of God's people. This intense persecution continued *even to the time of the end:*

> *Dan11:33 And they that understand among the people shall instruct many: yet they shall fall by the sword, and by flame, by captivity, and by spoil, many days . . .* ³⁵*And some of them of understanding shall fall, to try them, and to purge, and to make them white, even to* <u>the time of the end</u>*: because it is yet for a time appointed.*

In the *chêzêv* of Daniel 7, there is also a record of the persecuting power of a little horn:[77]

> *Dan7:24 And the ten horns out of this kingdom are ten kings that shall arise: and another shall rise after them; and he shall be diverse from the first, and he shall subdue three kings.* ²⁵ *And he shall speak great words against the most High, and shall wear out the saints of the most High, and think to change times and laws: and they shall be given into his hand until a time and times and the dividing of time.*

This idiomatic phrase, time, times and the dividing of time[78] has been widely accepted as equaling three and a half

---

[77] Note: While the little horn power of Daniel 8 describes Rome in both its pagan and papal phases, the little horn power of Daniel 7 more properly describes Papal Rome.

[78] עִדָּן, 'iddân, id-dawn'; (Aramaic) from a root corresponding to that of H5708; a set time; technically, a year:—time. Strong's Concordance with

years.[79] The narrative suggests that it is to be marked with the direct persecution of God's people and associated with a little horn power. This little horn power would persecute God's people for such a period _even to_ the _"time of the end"_:

> _Dan11:35_ _And some of them of understanding shall fall, to try them, and to purge, and to make them white, even to the time of the end: because it is yet for a time appointed._

These portions of the narrative, Dan 11:33, 7:24 and 11:35 speak of an entity that comes into existence subsequent to the establishment of the fourth beast / kingdom i.e., after the conquest of Grecia; yet, being a part of this fourth kingdom.[80] Mention must here be made as a reminder that this fourth kingdom was a divided kingdom. Now, after the ten horns, i.e., after the breakup of the fourth kingdom, a little horn uproots three and wears out the people of God for _a time, and times and the dividing of times._ It is this same little horn that now persecutes _"them of understanding"_, until _"the time of the end"_.

Now this same persecuting little horn is the same king mentioned here in Daniel 11:36,[81] which speaks marvelous things against the God of gods:

Hebrew and Greek Lexicon, accessed July, 15, 2020, https://www.blueletterbible.org/ lang/Lexicon/ Lexicon.cfm?strongs= H5732 &t=KJV.

[79] Note: This phrase, time, times and the dividing of times is also at times expressed as (time, 360 + times, 720 + dividing of times, 180) equaling 1,260 days.

[80] Note: Both Pagan and Papal Rome are described as little horns. Both grew up from its littleness to become a power to be reckoned with.

Dan11:36 And the king shall do according to his will; and he shall exalt himself, and magnify himself above every god, and shall speak marvellous things against the God of gods, and shall prosper till the indignation be accomplished: for that that is determined shall be done. 37 Neither shall he regard the God of his fathers, nor the desire of women, nor regard any god: for he shall magnify himself above all.

This king/little horn is spoken of as being diverse i.e., it has characteristics that are horizontal and vertical. Horizontally, it is the only power that persecutes/wears out God's people for a *time, times and the dividing of times.* Vertically, he attacks the very God of the universe, regards no god; but magnifies himself above all, i.e., making himself god.

Another level of complexity added to the narrative of Daniel 11 is brought about by the change from specific entities to symbolic entities. While Daniel 11:1-4 speaks of entities in literal terms, beginning with Daniel 11:5, symbolic entities are referenced.

Dan11:5 And the king of the south shall be strong, and one of his princes; and he shall be strong above him, and have dominion; his dominion shall be a great dominion.

In this portion of the narrative, Daniel 11: 1-14, the symbolic entities being spoken of are on the horizontal plane, they are physical entities. The narrative speaks of the nation of Egypt and

---

[81] Note: As noted in the *châzôwn* of Daniel 8, the symbol used to denote the kingdom that comes subsequent to the he-goat (Greece) was a little horn. In Daniel 11, this little horn power would be described beginning at v14 as the robbers/breakers of thy people (Pagan Rome) and continuing afterward as one that exalts themselves. This description continues to v45.

the Ptolemys whose wars with Syria and the Seleucids are well documented. Subsequently, although the king of the North changes to Rome, i.e., *the robbers of thy people* and its wars with Egypt, the symbolism is yet on a physical/horizontal plane. However, when the direction of the narrative changes from a horizontal plane to a vertical plane, (v30) the symbolism no longer remains on a horizontal plane; but it transcends to symbolisms on a vertical plane.

On the horizontal plane, Pagan Rome fell because of the invasions of the various barbarian tribes from the north and the abdication of its last emperor in 476ad. While heretofore, there had been one unified, geographically contiguous empire, it is now broken into pieces and the nations of Europe were born upon the territory once held by Western Rome. On the vertical plane, the bishop of Rome rose to become not only the sole ecclesiastical power, but also stepped into the political vacuum created by the abdication of the last emperor. In 533ad, Justinian, Emperor of the Eastern Roman Empire decreed upon the Bishop of Western Rome the title, corrector of heretics.[82] The Papacy was now an ecclesiastical entity clothed with civil power, whose rule would fulfill the *time, times and dividing of times* unto *"the time of the end"*.

Following the trajectory of the *chêzêv* of Daniel 2 and 7 and the *châzôwn* of Daniel 8, for which Daniel 9-12 provides a portion of the interpretation, the fourth kingdom would be divided and broken into several nations. After uprooting three, a little horn would take prominence and remain until the coming of the Lord.

---

[82] Note: This decree, although made in 533ad, was not actualized until 538ad, when Pope Vigilus became the head of all the churches in Rome, both east and west.

This little horn/king of fierce countenance/King of the North (Daniel 11:30-45) is Papal Rome.[83] This entity after being endowed with ecclesiastical and political power would retain dominance for three and a half years of prophetic time, while persecuting God's people for the said period. This period in prophetic days is the same as 1,260 days. When translated to years and added to 538ad would terminate in 1798ad. History bears record that in 1798ad, Napoleon Bonaparte, while intending to unify Europe, sent General Berthier into Rome and arrested Pope Pius VI thereby ending the long stretch of power that was once touted as the Holy Roman Empire.

Note that in the narrative, once the vertical trajectory takes center stage, there is no attack from the King of the South until the time of the end. Needless to say, that there were several wars on a horizontal plane after the Bishop of Rome took office in 538ad; however, because the narrative shifted from horizontal to vertical, the Papacy remained unchallenged on a vertical plane until *the time of the end* when the King of the South shall נָגַח, push[84] at him. This push carries the very same connotation of Daniel 8:4 when the ram was seen pushing westward, northward and southward so that no beast could stand before him. This push is an act of war

---

[83] Note: Papal Rome is also depicted as a little horn as its origin was at first confined to an individual, the office of the bishop of Rome; however, after the abdication of the last emperor, the bishop of Rome stepped into the vacuum created and became both the ecclesiastical and as well as the political leader of the Western Roman Empire.

[84] נָגַח, nâgach, naw-gakh'; a primitive root; to butt with the horns; figuratively, to war against:—gore, push (down, -ing) Strong's Concordance with Hebrew and Greek Lexicon, accessed Oct, 19, 2020, https://www. blueletterbible.org/ lang/Lexicon/ Lexicon.cfm?strongs=H5055&t=KJV.

between two entities, the King of the North being the Papal Rome and the King of the South.

Throughout Daniel 11. The King of the South has ever been Egypt; however, when the symbolism changed from the horizontal to the vertical, it would become symbolic of that entity, which fitly represents Egypt on a vertical trajectory:

> *Ex5:1 And afterward Moses and Aaron went in, and told Pharaoh, Thus saith the LORD God of Israel, Let my people go, that they may hold a feast unto me in the wilderness. ² And Pharaoh said, Who is the LORD, that I should obey his voice to let Israel go? I know not the LORD, neither will I let Israel go.*

In this response to Moses and Aaron, Pharaoh depicted that which is representative of Egypt. A country that does not know God, i.e., an atheistic country/government. In the French Revolution of 1789-1799, France removed any semblance of God from itself and enthroned the "goddess of reason", a country without God. Thus, in the war at *the time of the end*, 1798, it was the symbolism of Egypt's vertical trajectory, atheism that pushed/gored/warred against the Papacy bringing an end to the longest reigning entity of the *châzôwn*. The *châzôwn* has now stretched over many days. Having been given in the 3ʳᵈ year of Belshazzar, its start point was given as the *going forth of the command to restore and build Jerusalem*, 457bc. It has now reached to *"the time of the end"*, 1798.

Once again, the embedded chapter break at Daniel 12 must be dismissed in order to connect and realize the full flow of Gabriel's unbroken interpretive speech narrative. This continued monologue is the substance of the entire Chapter 11 of Daniel with portions flowing into Chapter 12. Remember Gabriel's words at the end of Chapter 10, while talking with Daniel:

> *Dan10:21 But I will shew thee that which is noted in the scripture of truth: and there is none that holdeth with me in these things, but Michael your prince.*

Gabriel had promised Daniel to show him not only what shall befall Daniel's people in the latter days; but, also that which is noted in the Scripture of truth, which only Michael/Christ is more versed than he is.

Now, at the outset of Chapter 12 is found a verse that needs immediate redress:

> *Dan12:1 And at that time shall Michael stand up, the great prince which standeth for the children of thy people: and there shall be a time of trouble, such as never was since there was a nation even to that same time: and at that time thy people shall be delivered, every one that shall be found written in the book.*

The time here spoken of, when *Michael shall stand up to deliver Daniel's people, every one that shall be found written in the book,* is that time, which was mentioned in the chapter just prior as, *the time of the end:*

> *Dan11:40 And at the time of the end shall the king of the south push at him: and the king of the north shall come against him like a whirlwind, with chariots, and with horsemen, and with many ships; and he shall enter into the countries, and shall overflow and pass over.*

The *time of the end* is for an appointed time (Dan 11:35). That is to say it has a beginning. It begins at a predictable time, 1798.

This phrase, however, does not denote the end of historic time. There are events that occur in *the time of the end* and before the end of historic time, such as the king of the South's push at the King of the North and the subsequent retaliation. In *"the time of the end,"* there is also *a time of trouble such as never was, since there was a nation.* Michael standing up and delivering those who are found in the book, connotes a judgment[85], at *the time of the end,* especially in light of ch12:2 that speaks *to everlasting life and everlasting contempt.* It can therefore be said, *the time of the end,* which begins at the end of *the time, times and dividing of time ,* 1798 includes a judgment, i.e., the standing up of Michael and the deliverance of every one that is found in the book, some to everlasting life and some to everlasting contempt and continues until to the end of historic time.[86]

---

[85] Note: this judgment takes place at *"the time of the end* and before the end of historic time. The end of historic time can be understood as being synonymous with the Second Coming of Jesus.

[86] Note: At the Second Coming of Christ, historic time will have ended.

13: How Long?

This study has now covered all the visual portions of the *châzôwn* and will now proceed to the auditory portion. While still in awe of Gabriel's unbroken interpretive speech narrative, Daniel looks around and sees that there are other heavenly beings present:

> *Dan12:5* *Then I Daniel looked, and, behold, there stood other two, the one on this side of the bank of the river, and the other on that side of the bank of the river.* *6* *And one said to the man clothed in linen, which was upon the waters of the river . . .*

Note carefully that this is the very same scene described at the outset of the *dâbar* portion of the *châzôwn*. Daniel 8:13 records two saints speaking one to another with ch8:15 mentioning the appearance of a man, who spoke, giving Gabriel a directive:

> *Dan8:16* *And I heard a man's voice between the banks of Ulai, which called, and said, Gabriel, make this man to understand the mar'eh [that which was seen].*

In the first scene, by a river, there is a conversation between two in the proximity of the River Ulai and one, like the appearance of a man between the banks of the River Ulai. There is a speech between the two and the man on the water gives the response. In the second scene, there are two on either side of the River Hiddekel and a man upon the water of the River Hiddekel. In all there are four heavenly beings in each scene, Gabriel being in both. Both speeches, in ch8:13 and ch12:6 commence with the question, "How long?" Undoubtedly, the substance of the *dâbar* portion of the *châzôwn* is about time, God's prophetic time. God has here, through the prophet Daniel, laid out His timetable of events that will enable every subsequent generation to understand the events that will occur on planet earth, which will happen and occur before and at *"the time of the end"*.

When dissected in the original language, the first "how long?" is expressed as follows:

> *Dan8:13 How long ~~shall be~~ the châzôwn ~~concerning~~ the daily ~~sacrifice~~, and the transgression of desolation, to give both the sanctuary and the host to be trodden under foot?*

Since the *"How long?"* pertains to each component of the question asked. By removing the inserted words, it can easily be dissected as follows:

How long?

(a) The *châzôwn*
(b) The daily and the transgression of desolation
(c) To give the sanctuary to be trodden underfoot
(d) To give the host to be trodden underfoot

> Because this was a compound question, each of these *"How long?"* constitutes a time component independent of itself:

(a) How long the châzôwn?
> *Dan8:17... Understand, O son of man: for at the time of the end ~~shall be~~ the châzôwn.*

> *Dan8:26 . . . shut thou up the châzôwn; for it ~~shall be~~ for many days.*

Dan9:24 Seventy weeks are determined[87] upon thy people and upon thy holy city . . . to seal up the châzôwn and prophecy.

Dan11:14 . . . also the robbers of thy people shall exalt themselves to establish the châzôwn; but they shall fall.

From the tenor of these references, a picture of the answer can be ascertained. The *châzôwn* itself is for *many days* and reaches *"the time of the end"*. It therefore covers all the visual elements presented in the *châzôwn* i.e., the ram, the he-goat and the little horn, which is the complete timespan of the kingdoms of Media-Persia and Greece, which includes all the events of the Maccabean period. It speaks of the fulfillment of the seventy weeks prophecy, which establishes the validity of the *châzôwn,* bringing the timeline to the periphery of Messiah. It details events in the iron monarchy of Rome and its division into its Pagan and Papal phases. The narrative of the *châzôwn* details God's timetable even to *"the time of the end"* and the standing up of Michael. The timespan of the *châzôwn* itself has therefore not yet reached its *terminus ad quim*, which is the end of historic time. It is then that Daniel's people would be delivered:

Dan12:1 And at that time shall Michael stand up, the great prince which standeth for the children of thy people: . . . and at that time thy people shall be delivered, every one that shall be found written in the book.

---

[87] Note: The meaning, here is, "seventy weeks are cut off".

(b) How long the daily and the transgression of desolation? Subsequent to this question asked in ch8:13, these desolating powers are mentioned jointly on only two other occasions:

> *Dan11:31* *. . . and shall take away the daily* ~~sacrifice~~[88], *and they shall place the abomination that maketh desolate.*

> *Dan12:11* *And from the time that the daily* ~~sacrifice~~ *shall be taken away, and the abomination that maketh desolate set up,* ~~there shall be~~ *a thousand two hundred and ninety days*

In the first instance in ch11:31, it speaks of an event, 'the taking away of the *daily* and the setting up the *abomination that maketh desolate'*. In the second instance, in ch12:11 it speaks of a length of time from this event that measures *a thousand two hundred and ninety days*.

This second instance in ch12:11 was in conjunction with the second "How long?" that was asked in ch12:6:

> *Dan12:6* *And* ~~one~~ *said to the man clothed in linen, which* ~~was~~ *upon the waters of the river, How long* ~~shall it be to~~ *the end of these wonders?* *7 . . .* ~~it shall be~~ *for a time, times, and an half; and when he shall have accomplished to scatter the power of the holy people, all these* ~~things~~ *shall be finished.*

---

[88] Note: Sacrifice is an inserted word and must not be used to investigate this answer.

The wonders here spoken of are concurrent with Gabriel's unbroken interpretive speech narrative, which reaches even to the end of historic time. The answer here given by the Man upon the river, while swearing by Him that liveth forever, is divided into two distinct components, *a time, times, and an half,* (1,260) which reaches to a determined period, *the time of the end* and an undetermined period, the scattering of the holy people, which reaches even to the *end of historic time.* So, these wonders will continue even until Michael stands up and everlasting life or contempt is pronounced upon all; but, the timespan of these wonders is punctuated by a determined period identified as *the time of the end.*

Here a distinction between these two timeframes (1,290 and 1,260) must therefore be understood. The length of time from the event, 'the taking away of the daily and the setting up of the abomination that maketh desolate' *shall be a thousand two hundred and ninety days;* however, at the identified punctuation, *these wonders shall be for a time, times, and a half* (1,260). The phrase used here is parallel with that used in ch7:25 where the saints would be persecuted by the little horn *for a time and times and the dividing of time.*

Both of these aforementioned timeframes (1,260 and 1.290) are predicated upon this second half of the fourth kingdom and therefore must have some overlap. This little horn/Papal Rome/King of the North (Daniel 11:30-45) are interchangeable symbols used of this same second half of the fourth kingdom. Here another symbol is used in conjunction with this second half of the fourth kingdom, the abomination of desolation. A timeline is hereby set in place from the setting up of this *abomination of desolation* that will not exceed *a thousand two hundred and ninety days*; while at the same time constrained by *a time, times and the dividing of times.* When Daniel heard this explanation and asked for clarification regarding these things/wonders, he was told that *the dâbâr are sealed till the time of the end.*

The takeaway is that *the abomination of desolation* is another symbol for the little horn, Papal Rome and the King of the North (Dan 11:30-45). This second half of the fourth kingdom would come to the end of its reign at the end of the 1,260 days,[89] i.e., *the time of the end*; however, from its setting up there would be a thousand, two hundred and ninety days. Since the 1,290 is bounded by the terminus of the 1,260, then its beginning must be prior to the start of same. Since the 1.260 ended in 1798, then the 1,290 must then begin in 508ad. It can therefore be accepted that the abomination of desolation, i.e., Papal Rome gained its momentum of strength against Pagan Rome in 508ad and that the *daily being taken away* symbolically speaks of Pagan Rome being displaced by Papal Rome.[90] The *abomination that maketh desolate* would then be Papal Rome. Think of it this way, the daily ~~sacrifice~~ being taken away, and the abomination that

---

[89] Note: Although the end of the reign of Papal Rome occurred in 1798, it still exists today and will continue until the end of historic time, as prophesied in the writings of Daniel.

[90] Note: In 508ad Clovis, king of the Franks was baptized into Nicene Christianity (Catholicism) from Arian Christianity, which was considered heretical. This became a major turning point for the routing of paganism (Arianism) and the forwarding of Catholicism in Western Rome.

maketh desolate being set up is an event. From this event until *the time of the end* there would be or *a thousand two hundred and ninety days, i.e., 1,290 years.* This began in 508ad and came to a close in 1798.

(c) How long to give the *qôdesh* to be trodden underfoot?

> *Dan8:14* *Unto two thousand and three hundred days; then shall the qôdesh be cleansed.*

> *Dan9:26* *and the people of the prince that shall come shall destroy the city and the qôdesh*

Subsequent to the "How long?" question in ch8:13 regarding the *qôdesh,* this word refers to the "sanctuary" only twice in the remainder of Daniel's writing[91]. In the first instance, he states plainly that after 2,300 days the *qôdesh* will be cleansed. In the second instance, he mentions that the people of the prince will come and destroy the city and the *qôdesh.* Since the question being asked is regarding the length of time whereby the *qôdesh* would be trodden down, ch9:26 would be disqualified to answer as it speaks to an event, to a destruction of the *qôdesh.*[92] Only ch8:14 provides an answer in regard to time. As previously shown, the 2,300 days would terminate beyond the seventy weeks of ch9:24.

---

[91] Note: Dan 8:13, 14 and 9:26 refers to the qôdesh as the sanctuary. In Dan 9:16, 20; 11:28, 30, 45 and 12:7 it refers to something or someone holy.

[92] This qôdesh that was destroyed is that which was mentioned in conjunction with the seventy weeks prophecy. It is a reference to the destruction of Jerusalem in 70AD.

Understanding that these 2,300 days must be calculated as years and begin concurrently with the seventy-weeks would find its terminus in 1844.[93]

(d) How long to give the host to be trodden underfoot?

> *Dan8:10 And it waxed great, ~~even~~ to the host of heaven; and it cast down ~~some~~ of the host and of the stars to the ground, and stamped upon them. [11] Yea, he magnified ~~himself~~ even to the prince of the host, and by him the daily ~~sacrifice~~ was taken away, and the place of his miqdâsh was cast down. [12] And an host was given ~~him~~ against the daily ~~sacrifice~~ by reason of transgression, and it cast down the truth to the ground; and it practised, and prospered.*

Whenever Daniel speaks of host, he uses the same word, which means a mass of persons. In the first interpretive segment of the *châzôwn,* Dan 8:15-27, Gabriel tells Daniel that the king of fierce countenance (little horn in the vision segment) *shall destroy the mighty and holy people* and that *by peace shall destroy many: he shall also stand up to against the Prince of princes.* (Dan. 8:24, 25). Under this same symbol of a little horn, God's people / *saints of the most high shall be given into his hands until a time, and times and the dividing of times. (Dan7:25).* This period of time terminates coincidentally with the *time of the end",* 1798. The host would therefore be trampled underfoot by the little horn for the duration of its reign,

---

[93] Note: See Chapter 8: Seal up the châzôwn for the details of this understanding.

1,260 years, i.e. Papal Rome would persecute God's people for the duration of it reign.

Returning to the questions asked in Daniel 8:13 by the heavenly beings and the subsequent unbroken interpretive narrative presented by Gabriel, (Daniel 11:1-12:3) note carefully that the answers to the questions cannot all be found in Daniel 8. Without the rest of Gabriel's unbroken interpretive narrative of the *châzôwn,* some questions would have gone unanswered. The answer given immediately in Daniel 8:14 only answers the question of how long the sanctuary would be trodden underfoot:

> *Dan8:14 And he said unto me, Unto two thousand and three hundred days; then shall the sanctuary be cleansed.*

Therefore, at the end of Gabriel's interpretive narrative, the second "How Long" is repeated so as to return to the questions first asked. Without the second "How Long?" the remaining questions from Daniel 8:13 would not be answered.

The question "How long shall be the *châzôwn?*" is alluded to in Daniel 8:17 as reaching to the time of the end:

> *Dan8:17 . . . Understand, O son of man: for at the time of the end shall be the châzôwn.*

However, this question is unpacked more fully in the second how long. "How long to the end of these wonders?" (Dan 12:6). The wonders here spoken of consist of the entire unbroken interpretive narrative, which concluded in Daniel 12:3. This interpretive narrative includes the standing up of Michael at *the time of the end* and the time of trouble such as never was. It includes the dead being raised to everlasting life and the wicked being banished into everlasting contempt, an allusion to the final judgment and the Second Coming of Christ. The full answer to the question of

"How long the *châzôwn*?" would then be, until the end of historic time. The *châzôwn* is God's timetable of events from the time of it being penned even until He returns!

Reflecting on Daniel 12:11:

> *Dan12:11 And from the time that the daily ~~sacrifice~~ shall be taken away, and the abomination that maketh desolate set up, ~~there shall be~~ a thousand two hundred and ninety days.*

It would seem as though this statement is out of place as in Chapter 12 there was no direct question that prompted this response; however, when understood, by virtue of the scenes set by the four divine beings by the rivers, which bookends the beginning and the end of Gabriel's interpretation of the *châzôwn*, the answer would be in response to the question asked at the beginning in Daniel 8:13, which was not then answered. The question: *"How long the daily and the transgression of desolation?"* The answer:

> *Dan12:11 And from the time that the daily ~~sacrifice~~ shall be taken away, and the abomination that maketh desolate set up, there shall be a thousand two hundred and ninety days.*

A thousand two hundred and ninety days is given for the length of days of the abomination that maketh desolate. This time would end in 1798.

The final question, *"How long to give the host to be trodden under foot?"* (Dan 8:13) is also answered in the question: *"How long to the end of these wonders?"* Note that answer is in two parts:

> *Dan12:11 . . . it shall be for a time, times, and an half; <u>and</u> when he shall have accomplished to scatter the power of the holy people, all these things shall be finished.*

Although the text answers the immediate question as to the length of time to the end of the wonders, it is demarked by a time period of time, times and a half. This cryptic phrase is directly mentioned in the *chêzêv* of Daniel 7:

> *Dan7:25* *And he [little horn} shall speak great words against the most High, and shall wear out the saints of the most High, and think to change times and laws: and they shall be given into his hand until a time and times and the dividing of time.*

Realizing that this cryptic timeframe is mentioned in conjunction with the persecuting little horn power, a complete picture can now be drawn. The host (God's People) shall be given to be trampled underfoot by the little horn more directly for 1,260 days/year; however, this persecution would continue afterward even into the time of the end and until Michael stands up at the end of historic time. It is then that these persecutions and wonders would end.

14: Last Words

It should be undeniably obvious that Daniel sought to understand the full meaning of that which he had heard in Gabriel's unbroken speech narrative. The response is consistent with the tenor of the *châzôwn*. The understanding was yet for many days, even to the time of the end:

> *Dan12:13* *But go thou thy way till the end be: for thou shalt rest, and stand in thy lot at the end of the days.*

A note in passing must here be made, Daniel was told that he would rest. Note it was not said of Daniel, who was so *"greatly beloved"* that Michael (Christ) Himself visited with him, that he would be transported into the bosom of Abraham where he would dwell in paradise; but that Daniel would rest in the grave. This statement directly confronts those who believe that their loved ones go directly to heaven at their passing.

The text also says that Daniel would stand in his lot at the end of the days. The question that must then be asked is, what is the lot of Daniel? For the answer to this question, we must examine the words of Jesus, Himself, who answered this question in the gospels of Matthew and Mark:

> *Matt24:15* *When ye therefore shall see the abomination of desolation, spoken of by Daniel the prophet, stand in the holy place, (whoso readeth, let him understand:)*

> *Mark:13:14* *But when ye shall see the abomination of desolation, spoken of by Daniel the prophet, standing*

where it ought not, (let him that readeth understand,) then
let them that be in Judæa flee to the mountains:

Daniel is a prophet! He is not a historian as scholars and biblical critics have portrayed him to be. Those who are Bible believing Christians should believe the words of Jesus over that of today's critics who portray the writer of Daniel as an inaccurate historian. And by standing in his lot *at the end of the days* would connote that Daniel's words that were shut up till *the time of the end* would become fully understandable after 1798.

There is one additional last word that must here be noted. In today's eschatological circles, there are many and varied compositions on the writings of Daniel. Aside from the biblical critics that seek to destroy the prophetic word that God has given to guide His people to the end of historic time, there are those who posit a different view that has herein been denoted. In one of these other views, the position taken is that Daniel's prophecies are relegated to a time past when King Antiochus IV Epiphanes, reigned as the 8th king of Syria. All the time prophecies that have been recorded in the book of Daniel is therefore, in one way or another connected to this Maccabean period.

In this view, termed Preterism, the *châzôwn,* along with Gabriel's interpretation is not recognized as one contiguous vision narrative that begins in Daniel 8:1 and ends at Daniel 12:13. Preterism breaks the *châzôwn* into three independent visions. Daniel 8 is one vision. Daniel 9 is another vision and Daniel 10-12 is a third vision. The challenge with accepting this view is that in Daniel 8, Daniel takes great pains to document the detail of his heavenly encounter. He uses a different word, *châzôwn* to describe this experience as unique from the others *(chêzêv)* that he had had previously. Note carefully, whenever Daniel has a vision, he describes it in detail.[94] However, in Daniel 9, there is no description of a new vision. Instead, Daniel makes reference to Gabriel by name as the one he had previously seen in the *châzôwn!*[95]

Additionally, the language of Gabriel in Daniel 9 demonstrates that his present encounter with Daniel is directly tied to the previous encounter in Daniel 8:

> *Dan9:24Seventy weeks are determined[96] upon thy people and upon thy holy city . . . to seal up the châzôwn and prophecy.*

As previously shown, these seventy weeks must be cut off from something greater, linking this seventy weeks' time-period to the two thousand three hundred days of Daniel 8. And finally, these seventy weeks seal up the *châzôwn and prophecy*, placing a portion of the *châzôwn* in the periphery of Messiah. The narrative of Daniel 8 and Daniel 9 are inextricably linked and cannot be separated. It has also been shown in this study that Daniel 10-12 is a continued exposition of the *châzôwn* along with the *dâbar* of Daniel 8, which reaches to the standing up of Michael and the establishment of the Kingdom of God. On these points the exposition of Preterism's eschatology fails.

Another view, Futurism and its corollary Dispensationalism also fails. This view posits, similarly that the *châzôwn* is broken into the same three visions as does Preterism; however, this view

---

[94] Note: See Daniel 2:19; 7:1; 8:1-3; 10:1-7.

[95] Note: It is only in the châzôwn of Daniel 8 that Gabriel is previously explicitly mentioned by name.

[96] "Seventy weeks are cut off".

accepts that sixty-nine of the seventy weeks prophecy of Daniel 9 terminates in the periphery of Messiah; however, the final week, which according to their eschatology is posited to begin and end concurrently with "the seven-year tribulation". This final week would end with the Second Coming of Jesus. The issue with this view is similar to that of Preterism in that there is no explanation regarding the seventy weeks being "cut off", nor does it account for the seventy weeks sealing up the vision and prophecy. Futurism provides no credible account for the two thousand three hundred days, except to relegate it to the Maccabean period. Futurism uses the English rendering of the word, "determined" to forward that the seventy weeks prophecy is determined/directed solely upon Israel and that portions of Daniel 9:24 are yet unfulfilled.

Additionally, Futurism and Dispensationalism posits that there is a gap in the prophetic timeline of the seventy weeks prophecy and that the sixty-ninth weeks have already occurred; but the seventieth week has not yet started. This they postulate, saying that all the items detailed in the seventy weeks prophecy, Daniel 9:24, have not yet been fulfilled. Following their line of reasoning, the seventieth week commences with the rapture of the church and terminates with the Second Coming of Jesus. The question that Futurism fails to answer is, how to account for the sealing up of the *châzôwn?* Remember that the seventy weeks unquestionably seals up the *châzôwn* and that the *châzôwn* is a time prophecy greater than the seventy-weeks itself. Now, according to Futurism / Dispensationalism the seventy weeks prophecy does not terminate until the Second Coming, therefore, the rest of the *châzôwn* from which the seventy weeks are "cut off" are yet unaccounted for.

The third of today's four major eschatological views, Idealism does not follow any historical timeframe. It is based on the idea that society will become better in the ensuing years; however, this flies in the face of Scripture:

> *2Tim3:1 This know also, that in the last days perilous times shall come. 2 For men shall be lovers of their own selves, covetous, boasters, proud, blasphemers, disobedient to parents, unthankful, unholy, 3 without natural affection, trucebreakers, false accusers, incontinent, fierce, despisers of those that are good, 4 traitors, heady, high-minded, lovers of pleasures more than lovers of God; 5 having a form of godliness, but denying the power thereof: from such turn away.*

The Bible clearly states that society will surely degrade in the latter days and not progress to any social utopia.

The final eschatological view, Historicism, does follow the structure of *châzôwn*. It is the view that is evident in the unbroken interpretive narrative of Gabriel. It is also evident in the words of Jesus and in this study:

> *Luke24:27 And beginning at Moses and all the prophets, he expounded unto them in all the scriptures the things concerning himself.*

This conversation must have included the events that underscored the prophetic and historical composition of Jesus, the Messiah. Of all the eschatological views used amongst biblical scholars today, Historicism is the one that has been around the longest. Historicism might not be the most popular view amongst today's eschatological adherents; however, Jesus never taught his disciples to follow the crowd:

Matt7:13 *Enter ye in at the strait gate: for wide is the gate, and broad is the way, that leadeth to destruction, and many there be which go in thereat:* *14* *because strait is the gate, and narrow is the way, which leadeth unto life, and few there be that find it.*

It is not the majority that will enter into the way that leads to life. It is the few who decide to follow the truth and not the popular. Jesus warns that before His coming there will be many false christs, false prophets and much deception. Truth seekers must follow the Scripture, thereby following after righteousness.

1John2:29 *If ye know that he is righteous, ye know that every one that doeth righteousness is born of him.*

15: Conclusion

Indisputably, the *châzôwn* has been given to underpin God's timetable from its conveyance until *the time of the end,* and beyond, even to the end of historic time. This timetable would not be fully understood until *the time of the end* had become evident. However, this understanding is not prevalent in today's eschatological circles. In actuality, this should not be a surprise to the careful student of Bible prophecy as Daniel in his presentation of events speaks of a power that will "think" to bring about an adulterated timetable of events. Speaking of the little horn of the fourth kingdom, Daniel states:

> *Dan7:25 And he shall speak great words against the most High, and shall wear out the saints of the most High, and <u>think to change</u> times and laws: and they shall be given into his hand until a time and times and the dividing of time.*

This verse acknowledges the antagonistic behavior between the little horn and God and God's people. The little horn will speak great words (blasphemy) against God; the little horn will wear out the patience of the saints of God. The little horn will think (it has the power) to change God's times and God's laws, and that God's people shall be given into the hands of the little horn for a *time, times and the dividing of time* (1,260 years)[97].

In the *châzôwn* God sets forth His timetable i.e., the flow of time and events that will transpire from the days of the kings of

---

[97] Note: See the systematic study, the *Visions of Daniel* for a complete exposé on this verse.

Media-Persia until everlasting life is bequeathed upon God's people and everlasting דְרָאוֹן, contempt[98] upon the others. This judgment motif can also be seen in the divine component of Daniel 7. More importantly, the imagery of the *châzôwn* intimates scenes of Israel's cultic practices observed during the Day of Atonement / cleansing of the sanctuary.[99] It is the only service in which rams and goats are used. This imagery coupled with Gabriel's statement that the sanctuary will be cleansed at the end of 2300 days present a judgment consistent with the divine component of Daniel's visionary experiences. This judgment would occur subsequent to the seventy weeks prophecy and subsequent to the *time, times and the dividing of time*, a metaphor that is consistent with *the time of the end*, 1798; however, note carefully that Michael stands up to deliver His people and not to judge them. This intimates that when Michael stands up the judgment has already occurred and He now comes to execute that which has been decided, those to everlasting life and those to everlasting condemnation.

In the *chêzêv* of Daniel 2, the prophet writes that God will set up His kingdom at the end of four earthly empires. In the *chêzêv* of Daniel 7, the prophet writes that at the judgment, the kingdom shall be taken from the little horn and given to the saints of the most High. In the *châzôwn* of Daniel 8-12, the same timetable of events is sequenced, and the sanctuary cleansed at the

---

[98] דְרָאוֹן, dᵉrâʾôwn, der-aw-one'; or דֵּרָאוֹן dêrâʾôwn; from an unused root (meaning to repulse); an object of aversion:—abhorring, contempt. Strong's Concordance with Hebrew and Greek Lexicon, accessed July, 15, 2020, https://www. blueletterbible.org/ lang/Lexicon/ Lexicon.cfm?strongs=H1860&t =KJV.

[99] Note: For a follow-on study of the sanctuary that is to be cleansed at the end of the two thousand three hundred days, please see the systematic study entitled, *The Sanctuary and its Cleansing.*

end of the two thousand three hundred days. These events, in the Hebrew half of Daniel, begin in the Media-Persia Empire and not in Babylon. This book, within the book of Daniel, particularly the *dâbar* was shut up and sealed until *the time of the end.* Daniel 9 presents the historic start event and start date of the *châzôwn,* and the sealing up of the *châzôwn,* consistent with the seventy weeks prophecy. Daniel 10 speaks of the great *mar'âh,* which Daniel had, wherein Michael was sent to assist Gabriel with issues during the Persian Empires. Daniel 11 provides the full flow of the *châzôwn* along with the *dâbar* with details of the King of the North and King of the South in both horizontal and vertical planes. It continues down to *the time of the end* and even till the end of historic time.

One of the final events recorded in the *châzôwn* is the Standing up of Michael and a time of trouble such as never was since there was a nation upon the earth. Note very carefully that the standing up of Michael is contemporary with this time of trouble. This standing up must therefore be understood as taking place prior to the Parousia (Second Coming) of Jesus. Michael stands up to deliver His people who are going through the time of trouble, *such as never was since there was a nation even to that same time:* (Dan 12:3) This *time of trouble* test is the final test to determine who are they that are on the Lord's side? God's people are not removed from experiencing the time of trouble, they are delivered out of it. The final event in the *châzôwn* is the judgment that rewards eternal life or contempt upon those who have lived on planet earth. Note also that this judgment takes place in *the time of the end* and not at the end of historic time, which is coincident with the Second Coming! It is the judgment and not the rapture that determines who will be found written in the book. These will be rewarded with everlasting life. Those not found will be rewarded with everlasting contempt. This event closes the *châzôwn.* This is

God's timetable of events that has been given to apprise individuals of events that will transpire before His return. Any other timetable, with regard to the *châzôwn,* especially if it is traced to the little horn/Papal Rome as its source, would be an adulterated version of God's eternal truths.[100]

---

[100] Note: See the systematic study, *Roots of Evangelical Lies* for a delineation of these adulterated version of God's timetable.

Bibliography

Anderson, Robert. *The Coming Prince*. Lawton, CA: Trumpet Press, 2012.

Anderson, Steven D. *Darius the Mede: A Reappraisal*. Scotts Valley, CA: CreateSpace, 2014.

Kaiser Jr., Walter C.; Garrett, Duane. *NIV, Archaeological Study Bible*, eBook. Zondervan. Kindle Edition.

Low, Alvin A. *Dreams and Visions: Decrypting the Book of Daniel*. Morrisville, NC: Lulu Press, 2018

Pope Leo XIII, *The Great Encyclical Letters of Pope Leo XIII* (New York, NY: Benziger Brothers, 1902).

Rabin, Elliot. *Understanding the Hebrew Bible*. Jersey City, N.J: KTAV Publishing House, Inc. 2006.

Strong's Concordance with Hebrew and Greek Lexicon, accessed October, 15, 2019, Retrieved from https://www.eliyah.com/lexicon.html.

Printed in Great Britain
by Amazon

27533293R00076